Australian
phrasebook

Denise Angelo, Carolyn Coleman & Melanie Wilkinson
Peter Austin & Barry Blake
Sue Butler
Alan Dench
Institute for Aboriginal Development
Dana Ober

Australian Phrasebook
  1st edition

Published by
  Lonely Planet Publications
  Head Office: PO Box 617, Hawthorn, Victoria, 3122, Australia
  Branches: 155 Filbert St, Suite 251, Oakland, CA 94607, USA
              10 Barley Mow Passage, Chiswick, London W4 4PH, UK
              71 bis rue du Cardinal Lemoine, 75005 Paris, France

Printed by
  Colorcraft Ltd, Hong Kong

Photograph by
  Front cover: Uluṟu, Northern Territory (Paul Steel)

Published
  October, 1994

National Library of Australia Cataloguing in Publication Data

  Australian phrasebook

  ISBN 0 86442 256 3.

  1. Australianisms. 2. English Language - Australia - Terms and phrases.
  [3]. Aborigines, Australian - Languages - Terms and phrases. 4. Torres
  Strait Islanders - Languages - Terms and phrases [5]. Aborigines,
  Australian - Languages - Conversation and phrase books - English. 6.
  Torres Strait Islanders - Languages - Conversation and phrase books -
  English. I. Angelo, Denise. (Series: Lonely Planet language survival kit).

427.994

Acknowledgements

The Australian English section of this book was written by Sue Butler. Many thanks to the various Aussie LP staff members for their comments, in particular Andrew Hewett who compiled the footy section whilst in the bath (the best place to think) and James Jenkin, linguist extraordinaire.

The Central Australian Aboriginal Languages chapter was compiled by Jenny Tindale from the Institute for Aboriginal Development, with contributions from Lizzie Ellis, Gavan Breen and Robert Hoogenraad, and ideas and assistance from Lorna Wilson, Mark MacLean and Ken Grime.

The Northern Australian Aboriginal Languages chapter was written by Denise Angelo, Carolyn Coleman and Melanie Wilkinson from the Katherine Regional Aboriginal Language Centre. Thanks to Murray Garde and Kuninjku speakers of Maningrida area for help with Kuninjku examples.

The Western Australian Aboriginal Languages chapter was written by Alan Dench. Barry Blake and Peter Austin wrote the chapter on the Aboriginal Languages of Victoria and New South Wales, and Barry Blake put together the Introductory chapter, with contributions from Jenny Tindale and Denise Angelo.

Dana Ober wrote the chapter on the Languages of Torres Strait. Thanks to Anima Ghee, Bakoi Pilot and Puitam Wees for contributions on their languages.

From the Publisher

This book was edited by Sally Steward. Maliza Kruh designed the book and drew the maps and illustrations. Jane Hart was responsible for the cover.

The languages in this book are the indigenous Australian languages, and English, the language commonly spoken by all Australians. As Australia is a multicultural country, there are also many community languages, which we have not been able to include, but we acknowledge their contribution to Australian culture.

Contents

AUSTRALIAN ENGLISH

INTRODUCTION 9
History .... 9 Australian Pronunciation 12

GENERAL AUSSIE ENGLISH 14
Aussie Informality .... 14 Shortened Forms 21
Meeting People .... 14 Clothes 25
Personal Names .... 16 Sports 26
Rhyming Slang .... 17 National Songs 28
Expressions 19

REGIONAL DIFFERENCES 31
Victoria .... 32 Queensland 39
New South Wales .... 33 Tasmania 40
South Australia .... 36 Australian Capital Territory 42
Western Australia .... 37 Other Regions 43
Northern Territory 38

BORROWED WORDS 45
US Influence .... 45 Aboriginal Influence 48
UK Influence 47

ABBREVIATIONS 55
The States & Territories .... 55 Acronyms & Abbreviations 56

FOOD & DRINK 60
Food in General .... 61 Children's Party Food 65
Meals .... 62 Hunger 65
Food You Might Encounter .... 63 Ordering Drinks 66
Tradenames .... 64 Pubs, Clubs & RSLs 67

THE AUSSIE PARTY 69
Drinking Protocol .... 70 The Bad Guys 75
The Argument .... 70 The Food 75
Temper .... 71 Inebriation 75
The Good Guys .... 73 Departure 76

THE CITY & THE BUSH 77
Country Places .... 77 Europeans & the Bush 79
Identifiable Regions .... 78 The City 82

ABORIGINAL LANGUAGES

INTRODUCTION **89**

Relatedness 90
Sounds 91
Vocabulary 93

Structure 93
Developments 94

CENTRAL AUSTRALIAN LANGUAGES **96**

Introduction 96
Keeping Languages Strong ..97
Talking with Aboriginal
People 98
Family Relationships 101
Travelling & Staying on
Aboriginal Land 103

Taking Photographs 104
Further Reading 104
Language Groups 105
Arrernte 105
Western Desert Language ..111
Warlpiri 116

NORTHERN AUSTRALIAN LANGUAGES **122**

Introduction 122
Historical Influences 123
Present-Day Situation 125
Kriol 127
Land Rights 128
The Languages 129

Katherine Region 129
Central Region 132
Daly Region 134
Darwin & the North Coast ...136
North-East Arnhem 138
Further Reading 141

WESTERN AUSTRALIAN LANGUAGES **143**

Introduction 143
Effects of European
Settlement..............................146
Keeping Languages Strong .147

Cultural Information 148
Specific Locations 150
Place Names 151
Further Reading 153

LANGUAGES OF VICTORIA & NEW SOUTH WALES **154**

Introduction 154
Victoria 156

New South Wales 158
Further Reading 159

TORRES STRAIT LANGUAGES **161**

Introduction 161
European Contact 163
Community & Cultural Life ..164
Specific Locations 167

Dialects of KLY & MM 167
Sounds & Pronunciation 168
Useful Words & Phrases 170
Further Reading 173

Australian English

Once a jolly swog
Camped by a Billabong
Under the shade of a Coolube

Introduction

History

What makes Australian English different from other Englishes in the world? Well — its history for a start. When the British Government established a convict settlement at Sydney Cove they had no thought for the linguistic consequences. As time went by, first the convicts then the settlers took English and adapted it to their new home, by twisting meanings of existing words or borrowing new ones to suit.

Convict Terms

Some words have filtered through from what was called the 'Flash Language' — the thieves' language of London — which became respectable on distant shores. For example, in London a *plant* was the name for stolen goods stashed away to be collected later when the coast was clear. In Sydney a plant came to mean stores and provisions stashed away in the bush to be collected on a return trip. To plant something was to put it away safely for later.

British English

Words of British English took on a whole new meaning in colonial circumstances. For example in the UK a *paddock* is a small enclosed meadow. In Australia a paddock can extend further than the eye can see. In the UK a *creek* is a small tidal inlet. In Australia a creek is a subsidiary of a river, which can be bigger than the Thames.

Aboriginal Words

An easy way for English to expand in Australia to meet the needs of the settlers was to borrow from the Aboriginal languages, particularly in describing the flora & fauna. Animals were named this way — the kangaroo, koala, wombat. Some plants are the mallee, the jarrah, the coolibah. Birds include the kookaburra, the currawong, the budgerigar; fish include the barramundi, the wobbegong and the yabby; among the reptiles are the perentie and the taipan. Some features of the environment are the billabong (a waterhole), the bombora (a treacherous current over a submerged rock), the willy-willy (a sudden twisting gust of wind).

The Goldfields

The growth of the goldfields in the 1850s brought an influx of people from all over the world. There are some words which have survived from the diggings, words like *fossick* which meant to dig through a heap of dirt for any leftover gold, and which now means to go carefully through anything in order to find something. The word *digger* itself referred at this stage to a miner, and since miners for very practical reasons always worked in pairs, the digger became the symbol of mateship in Australia, particularly in the emotional climate of WW I.

Twentieth-Century Australian English

The Federation of the Australian States which was formed on January 1, 1901, was a watershed in Australian history and separated a colonial society from a modern nation. There have been a number of significant milestones passed in this century which have all left their mark on Australian English.

WW I

Soldiers in this war contributed some slang to Australian English, such as a *furphy* (a rumour). Water was supplied to the soldiers in water carts made by John Furphy. The obvious place for the soldiers to exchange information of doubtful value was at the water cart, so these rumours came to be called furphies.

The Great Depression

The figure that emerged from the depression was the *battler*, the person who struggled against all odds. The battler was usually surviving on the *susso* (sustenance payments).

WW II

This war brought an influx of Americanisms, during and after it. But Australian army talk included words like *troppo* (mad as from too long a time spent in the tropics) and *spinebashing* (resting).

Contemporary Australian English

The influence of American English is very strong nowadays, particularly through the media. Australian children appear to be still resisting 'cookie' in favour of the Australian 'biscuit', and pronouncing **z** to rhyme with 'head' rather than 'bee', but they cheerfully refer to other people as dudes without any strong feeling that it is American.

Other currents that you might notice flowing in today's Australian English are the differences between the language of the older generation and the younger generation, and between the people who live in the city and those who live in the bush/country. It seems that much of the colloquial language in particular that is regarded as distinctively Australian might not be so popular with the younger generation living in the cities, who tend to take their fashionable colloquialisms from America.

Australian Pronunciation

Very early in the days of colonial settlement British visitors commented, usually disparagingly, on the Australian accent. Various attempts were made to correct the barbarous noises made by the locals from that early point in colonial history until comparatively recently. But the accent that formed among the children of the convicts, right back in the early days of settlement, has proved remarkably resistant to such efforts.

The Melting Pot Theory

The convict settlement included speakers of various British dialects whose accent remained much as it was when they landed on Australian shores. Being transported didn't change a Yorkshire man from being a Yorkshire man. There was no way that a Cockney convict was going to start sounding like his military masters. But the children of the convicts were like children anywhere — desperate to conform, desperate to win the acceptance of the other children. So with no particular prestige form of language to guide them, they forged a new accent of their own.

The Stranded Dialect Theory

The melting pot theory does seem to have a lot going for it, but there is an alternative theory to account for the Australian accent.

This goes along the lines that there was a predominant dialect amongst the convict community but this dialect is difficult to trace back to its British origins for two reasons. One reason is that while there is a conservative force operating in a colony that resists change, that force does not operate back in the mother country, where the dialect continues on its merry way leaving its previous form stranded in the colony.

The other factor which obscures identification is that some changes are forced on the colonial speakers by dint of circumstances. A strong competing dialect might bring about a few changes just by pressure of numbers of speakers and this can confuse the issue, making it harder to decide just what the original home dialect was, particularly when that dialect has also adapted in various ways.

Pronunciation Across Australia

It is noticeable that, despite the size of Australia, everyone apparently sounds the same. This is basically true — the only state that can claim a really different sound is South Australia, where the word 'school' (and others like it) is said with a clipped, shortened vowel that no other Australians can produce. But there are increasing claims for subtle differences that are becoming more pronounced. One distinctive pattern that has emerged amongst the younger generation is the rising statement — a statement such as 'It's a lovely day which ends in the kind of rising intonation usually reserved for questions.

General Aussie English

Aussie Informality

Being informal on any and every occasion is perhaps more important in Australia than anywhere else in the world. For the average Australian it says things about mateship, about equality, about the colonial escape from a class-ridden society. This means that we are more informal in our style of dress and in our style of speech more often, and more noticeably, in circumstances where in other countries formality would be expected. It is said of Australian English that it has a wide range of inventive and colourful slang and colloquialism. It is perhaps truer to say that the range of colloquialism is much the same as in any other language but Australians make more of it. Indeed they sometimes flaunt it.

Meeting People

Australians are known for their easygoing informality and friendliness. However it always helps to have a few of the basics of any language and the obvious starting point is how to say hello. G'day is the truly established Australian greeting but there are a few variations on this theme. This needs to be followed up with the appropriate goodbye.

Greetings

G'day.
Hi! or Hiya! (slightly suburban)
Yo! (younger generation)
How ya goin' mate – orright?
   (older generation – male)
How's tricks?
How are the bots biting?
   (bots are insects)

14

A general response to almost anything can be 'No worries'. To express appreciation, 'bonzer', 'ripper' or 'bewdy' will do fine.

Farewells

Catch-you-later, or Cop-you-later. (younger generation)
Ciao.
Hoo-roo. (old-fashioned)

Surprise

When Australians talk together, it's common for one to express basic astonishment at what the other is saying. It is good to be able to indicate that you are impressed even if this disguises total boredom, even if you have in fact stopped listening some hours ago. The following list is pretty much old-fashioned Aussie talk, but you may hear people say:

By cripes.
By jingo.
Crikey.
Struth.
Curl the mo.
Hell's bells.
Starve the bardies, starve the crows, starve the lizards.
Strike me lucky, strike me pink.

Disbelief

Occasionally it is necessary, it is even considered an important token of participation in the conversation, to express disbelief at what the other person is saying. An expression of mild disbelief is, after all, a way of giving them permission to say it all over again and so acts as a social lubricant. Once you have done your bit you can settle back to thinking about other things, doing the crossword puzzle, consulting the travel itinerary, whatever! However if the true blue Aussie is totally outraged by what is being told them, then go for the strong disbelief and prepare to engage in battle.

Mild Disbelief

Go on!
Get away with you!

This may be when you'll hear 'You haven't got a Buckley's', which means 'You haven't got a hope', 'You haven't got a chance, no way'.

Strong Disbelief

Bullshit, bulldust, bullcrap!
Pigs! or Pig's arse!

Extended Disbelief

Pigs might fly!
Pull the other one— it's got bells on! (referring to legs)
Don't come the raw prawn with me!

Personal Names

Australians are always keen to change names into diminutive forms, in the same way that they like to change *all* words into diminutives. Most famous Australians are affectionately known by 'ee' versions of their names (Jimmy Barnes is known as Barnsey, Kylie is always Kylie) although, oddly, names that do end in an 'ee' sound are often transformed into something else again.

Barry	*Bazza*	Murray	*Muzza*
Gary	*Gazza*	Sharon	*Shazza*

Rhyming Slang

Rhyming slang is an inheritance from London English, the language of the cockneys. Some of it has been brought from England, some is all our own. There are still some people who are addicted to rhyming slang, but the community as a whole operates successfully without it, apart from the odd fragments which have become embedded in the language.

barmaid's blush
> is a flush in poker. It also refers to a drink made from port wine and lemonade, or rum and raspberry.

amster
> is an old-fashioned word for a person who tries to drum up business outside a sideshow (the rhyme is 'Amsterdam' ram, a British word for the same kind of showman). Also known as a 'spruiker', 'urger', 'drummer'.

butcher's
> is a look (the rhyme is 'butcher's hook' look). Have a butcher's at this, you say. Don't confuse this one with the following:

butcher's
> is feeling sick (the rhyme is 'butcher's hook' crook, sick). When you have the 'lurgi' (some vague unidentifiable illness, usually one that is definitely going around), then you feel butcher's.

China
> is an old-fashioned word for a friend (the rhyme is 'China plate' mate)

dropkick
> is an obnoxious person (the rhyme is 'dropkick and punt', a cunt)

loaf
> is your head (rhymes with 'loaf of bread'). 'Use your loaf' is an encouragement to someone to think rather than to cut some sandwiches.

Pommy
> is a Brit, that is, a person of British nationality and usually Anglo-Celtic extraction (the rhyme is 'Pomegranate', immigrant). Often shortened to Pom.

reginalds
> is underwear (the rhyme is 'Reginald Grundies', undies, from Reg Grundy, a well-known TV entrepreneur). Also known as 'reggies'.

scarper
> is to go away, usually at high speed or with some urgency (the rhyme is 'Scapa Flow', to go)

septic
> is an American (the rhyme is 'septic tank', Yank). Also shortened to 'seppo'.

Other Rhyming Slang

after darks	sharks
aristotle	bottle — also, arra
babbler	cook — also, babbling brook
Bob Hope	soap/dope (marijuana)
Captain	look (the rhyme is 'Captain Cook')
comic-cuts	guts
Dad & Dave	shave (Dad & Dave were pre-WW II cow-cockies)
dead horse	sauce, usually tomato sauce
hammer	back (the rhyme is 'hammer and tack')
hey-diddle-diddle	piddle
hit-and-miss	piss
Jimmy Britts	shits
Jimmy Dancer	cancer
Joe Blake	snake
Richard the Third	turd

Mickey Mouse	grouse (excellent)
Noah	shark (the rhyme is 'Noah's ark')
on one's pat	alone (the rhyme is 'on one's Pat Malone')
onka	finger (the rhyme is 'onkaparinga' the name of a kind of woollen rug)
optic	look ('optic nerve' – perve or look)
warwicks arms	(the rhyme is 'Warwick Farm' arm, from a well-known racecourse in Sydney)

Expressions

The little expression 'like a ...' opens a world of possibilities in the Australian context. Some of the more well-known or remarkable comparisons are as follows:

like a cut snake
is in an angry fashion. The snake in this case is cut or castrated and is understandably upset.

running around like a chook with its head cut off
is to be making a lot of commotion but not getting anywhere. This is the ultimate in pointless activity. The image goes back to that scene by the chopping block where the chook (chicken) which has been selected for dinner gets its head cut off. There is a moment when the chook, though decapitated, continues to run around until the message finally gets through to the muscles that whatever point there was in the chook's life isn't there any longer.

looks like a dog's breakfast
refers to anything that is in a dreadful mess. Breakfast should be an orderly affair, but a dog of course has things all over the place.

like a stunned mullet
> is in a completely dazed state, from various causes. Big fish are knocked over the head and the mullet is a pretty common fish to catch so perhaps its dazed expression has become familiar. Or perhaps it is because it is not uncommon to see the mullet before they begin to run hanging motionless in the water, totally uninterested in juicy worms or in anything else.

feel like a greasespot
> is to feel hot and sweaty, about to dissolve into a pool of grease

need (something) like a hole in the head
> is an ironic statement, for obvious reasons

go down like a lead balloon
> is to be a complete failure

go through like a dose of salts
> if something goes through you like a dose of salts, then it has the same effect on you as a purgative. But if you go through other people like a dose of salts, then you visit them for a brief period of time but with noticeable effect.

Phrases Expressing Various States of Being

- anger — mad as a meataxe, mad as a cut snake, mad as a frilled lizard, mad as a maggot
- insanity — mad as a gumtree full of galahs, mad as a mother-in-law's cat, mad as a hatter (a prospector who worked alone and suffered from isolation in the bush), silly as a two-bob watch, silly as a bagful of worms, silly as a wheel
- sadness — miserable as a shag on a rock, miserable as a bandicoot
- happiness — happy as a bastard on Father's Day, happy as Larry (possibly after the noted Australian boxer Larry Foley, 1847-1917)

- crudeness   rough as guts, rough as a goat's knees, rough as bags, rough as a pig's breakfast
- weakness   weak as piss, weak as water, weaker than a sun-burned snowflake
- dryness   dry as a bone, dry as a nun's nasty, dry as a pommy's towel (the British being known as never having a bath), dry as a dead dingo's donger
- fullness   full as a goog (egg — can also mean drunk), full as a footy final, full as a state school hat-rack, full as a tick, full as a boot, full as a bull's bum

Shortened Forms

Australians are fond of cutting their words down to size, usually by taking the first part of the word and finishing it off at an appropriate point with **-ie** or **-o**. This can be just for the sake of general efficiency (why say Communist when you could say Commie) or to indicate affection (the kids can in a rare moment of geniality be referred to as the kiddies, or even more playfully, the kiddie-winks). The **-ie** ending can be used to create a useful noun where no noun existed before, just an adjective. Thus from green we get the greenie, the person concerned with the environment. The **-o** ending is more neutral than the **-ie** one, and can be used to convey a certain nonchalance. Calling an American a seppo possibly conveys a more offhanded and distant attitude than calling him a septic does.

Affection & Generally Positive Attitudes

goodies, freebies, prezzie, kiddie, Aussie, chappie, hollies, littlies, youngie

Neutral -ies

alkie	an alcoholic
barbie	a barbecue
bikie	a motorbike rider
boatie	a person who sails boats, especially for recreation
brekkie	breakfast
brickie	a bricklayer
budgie	a budgerigar (small bird)
Brissie	Brisbane
cabbie	a cabdriver
cardie	a cardigan
caulie	a cauliflower
chalkie	a schoolteacher
chewie	chewing gum
chockie	a chocolate
Chrissie	Christmas
ciggie	a cigarette
cockie	a cockatoo
coldie	a cold bottle or can of beer
Commie	a Communist
conchie	a conscientious person, particularly a conscientious objector
cossie	a swimming costume
druggie	a drug addict
flattie	a flat-heeled shoe, or a flathead (the fish)
frenchie	a condom
frostie	a cold bottle or can or beer
gladdie	a gladiolus
greenie	an environmentalist
hottie	a hotwater bottle
jarmies	pyjamas

lippie	lipstick
maggie	a magpie (the bird)
meanie	a mean person
muddie	a mudcrab
mossie	a mosquito
oldies	one's parents
pollie	a politician
possie	position
postie	the person who delivers the mail
premmie	a prematurely born baby
quickie	a quick go at anything
rellies	one's relatives
rollie	a roll-your-own cigarette
sammie	sandwich
sandie	a sand crab
shrewdie	a shrewd person
sickie	a day off sick
smoothie	a smooth talker, or a style of drink made with blended fruit
sunnies	sunglasses
swiftie	a trick. To 'pull a swiftie' is to put one over someone.
Tassie	Tasmania
tinnie	a can of beer
townie	a town person
truckie	a truckdriver
U-ie	a U-turn in a motor vehicle
umpie	the umpire
undies	underwear
uni	university
vegies	vegetables

Vinnies	St Vincent de Paul's op shop (St Vincent's being a similar organisation to the Salvation army
weakie	a weak person
wharfie	a wharf labourer
wheelie	a manoeuvre performed on a bike or motorbike, in which the front wheel is lifted off the ground
Windies	the West Indian cricket team
Woolies	Woolworths (shop)
woollies	woollen clothing
yachtie	a person who loves sailing yachts

It is not unusual to find words ending in **-ie** also spelled with a **-y** ending. Thus a cabbie could well be a cabby. However some always take **-ie** and others seem always for some inscrutable reason to take **-y**.

backy	tobacco
Bundy	Bundaberg
comfy	comfortable
dunny	toilet
Esky	a large insulated box for keeping food and beer cold
footy	football
kindy	kindergarten
lavvy	lavatory
placky	plastic
telly	TV

There is the same kind of overlap between words ending in **-ie** and words ending in **-o**. Some can be either, some are always one or the other. The following always take **-o**:

ammo	ammunition
arvo	afternoon
compo	compensation
demo	demonstration
dero	a derelict person, a person who wanders the streets
garbo	a garbage collector
info	information
intro	introduction
lesso	lesbian
nasho	a young man doing national service (now defunct)
muso	musician
myxo	myxomatosis (an introduced disease which kills rabbits)
porno	pornography
rego	car registration
Salvo	member of the Salvation Army
secko	a sexual pervert
smoko	a break to have tea, coffee, perhaps a cigarette
speedo	speedometer
wino	an alcoholic given to drinking cheap wine

Clothes

Akubra	famous brand of Aussie hat
bathers	swimsuit (Vic)
cozzie	swimsuit (NSW)
daks	men's trousers
Driza-Bone	famous brand of Aussie raincoat
strides	men's trousers
thongs	rubber sandals, flip flops
togs	swimsuit (Qld)

Sports

barrack   to cheer on a team at a sporting event
caaarn!   typical cry, meaning 'come on'!
sunbake   sunbathing - not really a sport but a national pastime, often during cricket matches

The main sports in Australia are footy and cricket. Some of the footy teams are household names, as are some of the players.

Australian Rules Football

Mainly played in the southern states, though there is now a national competition. Played from autumn to spring on an oval up to 200 metres from end to end. Four posts at each end: two inner, taller ones called goal posts, two smaller, outer ones called behind posts. Teams of 18 (plus three interchangeable players on each side) aim to kick an oval ball cleanly between the goal posts and score a goal (six points). If the ball is touched on its way, or touches the post, or goes between a goal post and a behind post, it's worth a behind (one point). Scores of 20 goals or more by one or both teams are common. There are four quarters of 25 minutes each. The winning team is the team with the highest numbers of points at the end of the game, with drawn games being quite rare. Tackling is fierce, with only tackling above the shoulder or round the legs banned. If the ball is kicked and goes through the air for more than 10 metres and is then caught, this is called a mark and the player is awarded a free kick. Throwing the ball is barred, but a hand pass — holding the ball in the palm of one hand and hitting it with a clenched fist — is legal.

The Positions: full back line (two back pockets and one full back), half back line (two half back flankers and one centre half back), centre line (two winners and one centre man), half forward line (two half forward flankers and one centre half forward), full forward line (two forward pockets and one full forward) plus a ruckman, a ruck rover and a rover

Best-Known Venues: the MCG (Melbourne Cricket Ground), Football Park (Adelaide), Subiaco (Perth), WACA (West Australian Cricket Association, Perth), Princes Park (Melbourne)

Major Annual Event: AFL (Australian Football League) Grand Final, September, attended by over 100,000 and watched on TV by millions. Also the presentation of the Brownlow Medal to the player judged best and fairest by the umpires over the whole season.

AFL Teams: the Adelaide Crows, the Blues (Carlton), the Demons or Ds (Melbourne), the West Coast Eagles (Perth), the Sydney Swans, the Bulldogs (Footscray), the Magpies or Pies (Collingwood), the Tigers (Richmond), the Bombers (Essendon), the Hawks (Hawthorn), the Cats (Geelong), the Bears (Brisbane), the Lions (Fitzroy), the Kangaroos (North Melbourne), the Saints (St Kilda)

Slang Terms: white maggot (umpire), carn... (as in, carn the Blues – come on the Blues), speckie (spectacular high mark), coat hangered (hit by a straight arm), dragged (taken off the field)

Ball Kicks: There are many ways of kicking the oval-shaped ball: drop punt, drop kick (out of fashion kick, but in fashion term of verbal abuse), torp, screwie, checkside or banana kick, stab pass, mongrel punt, hospital ball, lean back and go bang, set sail for home, and a rain maker

Football Identities: Ron Barassi, Ted Whitten, Kevin Sheedy, Tom Hafey, Bob Skilton, Kevin Bartlett, Michael Tuck, Leigh Matthews.

National Songs

The Australian National Anthem is *Advance Australia Fair*. Most Australians don't know the words and mumble after the opening lines. The song you should really know and understand is the unofficial national anthem, *Waltzing Matilda*. The words are as follows:

Once a jolly swagman camped by a billabong
Under the shade of a coolibah tree,

The swagman is a tramp or itinerant who carries his swag, his bundle of clothes, cooking implements, etc, tied up in a blanket or bedroll. The billabong is a waterhole, most often found in the old bed of a river. The coolibah tree is a species of eucalypt found in inland Australia, often in areas which get flooded from time to time (hence the location near the billabong).

And he sang as he watched and waited till his billy boiled
You'll come a-waltzing Matilda with me.

The billy is a tin container used especially for boiling water for tea. No one is quite sure where the word comes from but it is probably from the Scottish *bally,* meaning pail or bucket. No one is quite sure about the origins of the expression 'waltzing Matilda' either but it probably dates back to a German influence on the goldfields mixing pot. The German equivalent of a swag is Matilda, the girl a man sleeps with when he is on the road and doesn't have a girl. And the expression 'to waltz' is used in the context of German apprentices moving from one town to another to learn their trade. The Germans in this case would have come from the Barossa communities in South Australia. Put together the phrase is the equivalent of being on the track, on the wallaby, on the road as a tramp.

> Down came a jumbuck to drink at the billabong
> Up jumped the swagman and grabbed him with glee
> And he sang as he shoved that jumbuck in his tuckerbag
> You'll come a waltzing Matilda with me.

The jumbuck is a sheep. This is thought to be Aboriginal pidgin for 'jump up', which is what the Aborigines presumably thought of as noticeable about sheep. The tuckerbag is the bag for food. Tucker is a British schoolboy word for food which still survives in Australian English. Great tucker! you can say, meaning good food.

> Up rode the squatter mounted on his thoroughbred,
> Down came the troopers one, two, three.
> Where's that jolly jumbuck you've got in your tuckerbag,
> You'll come a-waltzing Matilda with me.

This is the strong arm of the law arriving to arrest the swagman for stealing the jumbuck. Squatters were originally people who pioneered settlement on land the government hadn't got around to allocating yet. They unofficially squatted on land that they were not legally supposed to have. Eventually of course the government came around to their point of view and they became wealthy landowners, part of the squattocracy, the new aristocracy of pastoral Australia. This squatter rides a thoroughbred horse and can summon troopers (mounted police) to assist him.

> But the swagman he up and he jumped in the water hole,
>> Drowning himself by the coolabah tree;
> And his ghost may be heard as it sings in the billabong,
>> You'll come a waltzing Matilda with me!

Regional Differences

Regional Differences in Australian English

There are two schools of thought on this. One is anxious, some would say overanxious, to suggest that different regional dialects are emerging in Australia. The other says that Australia is remarkable for its linguistic uniformity.

The regionalists claim difference not just in the words we use but in the way in which we say them. You can tell a Melburnian from a Sydneysider they claim. Everyone can tell a Queenslander. And the South Australians can be picked as soon as they say 'school'. There may indeed be differences but they possibly amount to nuances of accent and community speech habits rather than a strong sound variation. But this is nothing like the difference between an Australian and a New Zealander, who simply has to ask for 'fush and chups' to be identified and whose English is travelling further along its own track with each generation.

As far as the words we use go, there are a few recorded regionalisms but not enough to cause much misunderstanding. And the way Australians move around the country a lot has meant that it is increasingly difficult to pin these down to one particular area. The regions in this case are based more on patterns of settlement from colonial days than on state boundaries. In many cases, when there is a difference, there will be a general word used by all Australians and then the particular regional word. In some cases, however, there is no standard word and we have to pick our way between the various regional uses.

Australians would like to be different. They pick over the items of regional variation with delighted fascination, sounding as if they can barely wait until the dialect of Adelaide is as remote from the dialect of Sydney as Scottish English is from a Yorkshire burr.

To look at the differences, we can divide Australia into the city or the bush, or we can examine it by region. An account of the regions is really an account of its big cities which are all, with the exception of the rather contrived city of Canberra, clinging to the coastline.

Victoria

the Cabbage Garden

Victoria was once known as the cabbage-garden because of the State's early ability to produce fruit and veg from its rich soil and accommodating climate. Victorians therefore were referred to as Cabbage Gardeners, the implication being that that is probably all they are good for.

Mexicans

Another way of looking at Victorians has been to describe them as Mexicans, that is, from the point of view of New South Wales they are south of the border.

Melbourne

Melbourne was named in 1837 by Governor Bourke after Lord Melbourne, then British Prime Minister. Melbourne is more English in its appearance and inclinations than any other capital city. Its residents claim to live stylishly – to eat well and to dress well, to be as sophisticated as Sydney is sleazy.

Melbourne also has trams – watch out for

'scratchies', the tickets which indicate if you have paid your fare. Do not confuse them with the other scratchies on which you get a chance to win the lottery. And be polite to the 'connie'— the tram conductor.

Victorian Lingo

Yarra banker

a soapbox orator on the banks of the Yarra

hook turn

a driving manoeuvre which terrifies the rest of Australia in which to turn right at an intersection you pull over to the left of the road with your right-hand indicator going, and then cross all lanes of traffic to negotiate the turn. Made necessary by the fact that the trams occupy the middle ground.

potato cake

what the New South Welsh would call a potato scallop. A slice of potato covered in batter and fried.

mudlark

known variously throughout Australia as the magpie lark, peewee or peewit. A medium-sized bird with black and white markings.

New South Wales

Cornstalks

New South Welshmen have sometimes been called cornstalks. It seems that quite early in colonial days the climate and way of life agreed with the newcomers so that the men who grew up in Australia became noted for their height and slim build. They grew like cornstalks, with the characteristic body tapering from broad shoulders to slim hips.

Sydney

Sydneysiders believe that Sydney is where it is at and that's all there is to say, a point of view which irritates the Melburnians in particular. But with the Bridge and the Opera House and one of the finest harbours in the world, and a generally hedonistic climate, who cares what the Melburnians say. Sydney was named by Governor Arthur Phillip (1738-1814) the British naval officer who brought the First Fleet to Sydney Cove, in honour of Thomas Townshend, 1st Viscount Sydney, who was Secretary of the Home Department at the time.

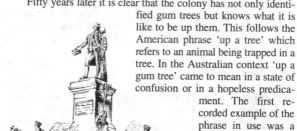

up a gum tree

apart from naming Sydney, Governor Arthur Phillip is the first person to have recorded the term 'gum tree' for a eucalypt in his journal of 1789. The name was thought apt because the substance oozing from the tree was thought to be a kind of gum. Fifty years later it is clear that the colony has not only identified gum trees but knows what it is like to be up them. This follows the American phrase 'up a tree' which refers to an animal being trapped in a tree. In the Australian context 'up a gum tree' came to mean in a state of confusion or in a hopeless predicament. The first recorded example of the phrase in use was a settler commenting on the behaviour of his workforce: 'My convicts were always drinking rum, I often wished they were up a gum-tree'. Employer/employee relationships in Australia have struggled to rise from this low point.

NSW Expressions

shoot through like a Bondi tram

some places are cultural icons — Bondi Beach is one of them. Australians have an image of this beach watched over by a kind of beach version of the Aussie digger, the Aussie lifesaver. At one stage, when Sydney had trams, there was a tram that went to Bondi. Apparently there was a stretch of the track near Centennial Park when the tram picked up speed and went noticeably fast. Nowadays, to shoot through like one is basically to bugger off.

up the Cross

if Bondi Beach is everything that is fine in life, then King's Cross is everything that is sinful. These days it is a little outclassed by Oxford Street, home of the annual Gay Mardi Gras, but to go up the Cross is still to enter a bohemian world.

the Coathanger

an irreverent name for the Harbour Bridge.

NSW Lingo

bubbler

what is more formally described as a drinking fountain

spider

fizzy drink, usually pink, with a dollop of ice-cream in it

lobster

what other people refer to as crayfish

devon

a kind of meat sausage, bland verging on tasteless

rockmelon

> this is known elsewhere as the cantaloupe. However the variety with pale green flesh is known as the honeydew everywhere.

South Australia

Croweaters

> South Australians have been known as Croweaters. The story behind this nickname is that life was so hard in South Australia that the colonials would very likely run short of sheep for the dinner table and be forced to eat crows. There's not much eating in a crow.

Adelaide

Adelaide is a pleasant town, well-heeled and respectable, easy to live in as a country town and as interesting as an international city. It is named after Queen Adelaide, the wife of William IV. It's biggest claim to being acknowledged as a city with big ideas is the Adelaide Arts Festival, a biennial affair which draws local and international talent.

South Australian Lingo

fritz

> also known as 'pork fritz'. This is the SA equivalent of devon. There is a strong German community near Adelaide.

donkey

> to give someone a ride on the back of your bike – what NSW people would call doubling.

butcher
  a small glass of beer.
echo
  a small beer bottle, like a stubby elsewhere, so called because
  it is returnable.

Western Australia

Western Australia is the largest state encompassing extremes of terrain and climate. As a result words like 'remote' and 'isolated' are likely to turn up as in terms like 'isolated child', 'isolated class', 'isolated school', 'isolated pharmacy', or 'remote posting', 'remote resident', 'remote site'.

Sandgropers
  Western Australians are called Sandgropers because most of
  the state is desert. To sand-grope is to walk in soft sand, a proce-
  dure that most people find tiring. Sandgroper is shortened to
  Groper. The Gropers of course live in Groperland.
Westralia
  Western Australia is sometimes referred to as Westralia so
  Western Australians are Westralians.

Perth

Perth is separated from the rest of Australia by the Nullarbor
Plain (Nullarbor being Latin *nulla arbor* meaning 'no tree').
Perth was named by Captain James Stirling after the city of the
same name in Scotland. On the whole people in Perth show no
sign of missing the rest of Australia, being entirely content with
the beautiful city they have and rather inclined to think on the
contrary that they would be better off without the rest of us. In-

deed West Australians refer to East Coast inhabitants as 't'other-siders' and 'Eastern Staters', and this is usually in tones of disparagement.

Western Australian Lingo

marron

a large freshwater crayfish, known elsewhere as yabbies

the doctor

the cool sea breeze which blows inland in the late afternoon and is identified variously depending on where you are. In Perth it is known as the Fremantle doctor because it blows into Perth from the direction of Fremantle.

Nyoongar

a West Australian Aborigine. (In a local Aboriginal language *nyungar* means 'man'.)

doublegee

the spiky seed of a common weed. It is also called 'Tanner's curse' and 'cat's head'. Elsewhere it is known as 'three-cornered jack' or 'spiny emex'.

polony

the bland cold sausage again. Remember devon?

skimpy

a scantily clad barmaid

Northern Territory

Top-enders

The inhabitants of the Northern Territory are known as Territorians, naturally enough, or as Top Enders, again naturally enough. A top end would presuppose a bottom end but this doesn't seem to happen. The only other place where the top end/bottom end distinction applies seems to be the Murray River where the bottom end is towards the mouth and the dividing line between top and bottom is marked by the conjunction of the Murray/Darling Rivers.

Darwin

Darwin was named after Charles Darwin, the English naturalist, who visited Australia aboard HMS Beagle in 1836. Darwin has always been the most multicultural of Australian cities. There has always been traffic amongst the islands to the north and the top end of Australia. The result of this is that Darwin has been eating laksa for years while it is relatively new on the menus of Sydney and Melbourne.

Northern Territory Lingo

the Wet
> the monsoon season

the Dry
> the opposite of the Wet. The final stage of this is referred to as 'the build-up' and causes great irritability amongst the inhabitants.

Queensland

Known as the Sunshine State, Queensland certainly has its fair share of sunshine and places in which to enjoy it. The coast is amiable but inland Queensland stretching up towards Cape York is as tough a strip of the outback as you will ever encounter. Towards the North is a region called the Channel Country in which numerous interlocking rivers regularly flood to form an inland sea.

Bananaland

Queensland is known as Bananaland and its inhabitants as Bananabenders, because of the big banana plantations on its south-eastern coast.

Brisbane

Brisbane was established as a convict settlement for the worst kind of offenders. It was named after Sir Thomas Brisbane, who was governor of NSW from 1821 to 1825. It is celebrated in song as a place of ultimate despair. Notwithstanding this grim past, it has emerged as a rather hedonistic city which can be a bit steamy in summer but which to compensate has the most beautiful clear, sunny winter.

Queensland Lingo

peanut paste

you'd think that Queenslanders as the peanut growers of Australia would have the last word on this, but peanut paste is peanut butter outside this state.

muddie

a Queensland mud crab – absolutely delicious

port

a request to bring a port in Queensland does not refer to a bottle but to a suitcase. It is short for 'portmanteau'.

Tasmania

Tasmanians feel they are often overlooked by the rest of Australia which they refer to as the Mainland, the inhabitants being Mainlanders. And certainly something seems to get lost in the translation over Bass Strait so that Tasmania and the rest of Australia are never quite on the same wave-length. Tasmania has some of the most beautiful scenery in the world and parts of it are still quite wild and inaccessible. The South Coast in particular where the Roaring Forties fetch up is remote, dangerous and beautiful.

Apple Island
 this name refers to Tasmania's past success in growing apples, although current crops don't feature the apple in quite the same way. The inhabitants are sometimes referred to as Apple Islanders.

Tassie
 an affectionate shortening of the name Tasmania is also a common name for Tasmania or a Tasmanian. Taswegian is another variation but not as common.

Hobart

Hobart is the second oldest city in Australia — the first convict settlement being at Sydney Cove and the second being established in Hobart in 1804. The city has an old-world charm — a fishing village character marked by Georgian houses and docks, with Mount Wellington towering above it. Hobart was named after Robert Hobart, fourth Earl of Buckinghamshire and Secretary of State for War and the Colonies (1801-04).

A rivalry exists between Hobart and Launceston which is similar to the tension between Sydney and Melbourne. So whatever Hobart gets, Launceston has to equal or do better.

Tasmanian Lingo

mutton bird

a species of shearwater which nests on islands off Tasmania and which is considered a gourmet item. It is extremely oily.

chalet

an outhouse or small dwelling in the arden of a main dwelling

cordial

Tasmanians and Queenslanders call a soft drink a cordial whereas elsewhere in Australia cordial is the sweet syrup used to make a non-fizzy sweet drink.

The Australian Capital Territory

The Australian Government Territory is the small area of land surrounding Canberra, the metropolis that is the capital city of Australia. As befits a government creation it hasn't really got any nicknames. Abuse yes, nicknames no.

Canberra

Canberra has the feel of a plush country town, the country town of your wildest dreams. It is a unique blend of town, gown and public service with politicians who zap in for the season in Parliament, and zap out again as fast as their planes can carry them.

The name 'Canberra' is an anglicisation of the Aboriginal name of the area. Walter Burley Griffin (1876-1937) an Australian architect born in the USA, created the original design of Canberra. People are still divided about the concept. Almost everyone agrees that they immediately get lost in Canberra, and some abuse has been hurled at Griffin by those who spend weary hours attempting to escape the endless loops and whirls that are Canberra's streetscape.

Canberra Lingo

govie/guvvie

a government-funded residence usually offering low rent. An ex-govie is one of these residences being offered on the open market.

Other Regions

There are a few other areas of Australia which emerge from the map as having a distinct identity.

The Riverina (or Sunraysia)

The lifeline of the Riverina is the Murray River, which feeds off the waters from the Snowy Mountains and then flows all the way to St Vincent's Gulf in South Australia. The area known as the Riverina is centred on Mildura and has sprung up around an irrigation scheme developed in 1923, which has made the dried fruit industry and vineyards of the region possible.

New England

New England, northeast of Sydney, is the district which claims the university town of Armidale as its centre. It is a farming and mining district – the name New England has to be seen as wishful thinking on the part of the settlers.

The Alice

This is the local name for Alice Springs, a town in central Australia in the southern part of the Northern Territory. Relatively close by is Uluru (formerly called Ayers Rock). Alice Springs was named after Alice Todd, the wife of Charles Todd who was responsible for the construction of the Overland Telegraph Line which connected Darwin to Adelaide and which was completed in 1872.

The Gold Coast

The strip of coastline just south of Brisbane is known as the Gold Coast. It is a tourist phenomenon — high-rise perched on the edge of the beach. It has been so successful that it is now rivalled by other 'coasts' — the Sunshine Coast (further north than the Gold Coast in Queensland) and the Capricorn Coast (the coastline near Rockhampton). New South Wales is divided into the South Coast (the Shoalhaven River to the Victorian border), the Central Coast (from the Hawkesbury River to Lake Macquarie) and the North Coast (from the Manning River to the Queensland border).

Borrowed Words

US Influence

The basic British influence in Australian English has been overlaid since WW II by a strong US presence, largely felt in the media. It is an indication of the speed at which American words can now move into Australian that it took only six months for couch potato to travel from the pages of a New York magazine (mild-1987) to a Melbourne newspaper (December 1987). Australians don't borrow everything that is new in American English – they take their pick. Among the popular US items which made it into Australian English in the '80s and '90s are:

bag lady
    an elderly woman who is homeless and who carries all her belongings in a shopping bag
bucket shop
    share brokers who go in for fast but questionable trade
cockamamie
    crazy; ridiculous; all muddled up
cornball
    a sentimentalist who is given to trite and hackneyed sayings
deep throat
    an anonymous informant within an organisation who leaks information to an outsider
dork
    a fool, particularly someone who is socially clumsy, dresses badly, and generally makes an idiot of himself. A dork is also called (but less commonly here) a 'dweeb'. Both these words are attempting to replace the Australian expression 'a dag'.
life in the fast lane
    this is '80s talk – at the height of yuppiedom life in the fast lane was where it was at

fast track
> to move something along in a process at unusual and irregular speed

kludge
> something improvised which does the job but in a clumsy and inelegant way

mover and shaker
> an important and influential person who makes things happen

parlay
> to convert a sum of money into an even larger sum by taking a gamble with it.

psychobabble
> the jargon of psychology, particularly that relate to psychotherapy groups

quiche eater
> a man who displays sensitivity in personal relationships and who can hold his own in discussions of social issues, particularly those that relate to feminism. He is viewed by some as effeminate, that is, as someone who spurns red meat and eats quiche instead.

spin control
> this is the kind of slant that can be given to anything that happens by the people who run the media campaign for a politician.

a tad
> means 'a little'. There is a theory that it is a shortening of 'tadpole' as applied to a small child.

underclass
> the people who are never caught up by society's safety nets and who form a class of their own with a lifestyle, culture and set of values entirely at odds with mainstream society

wimp
> a weak, effeminate, cowardly person. This word is being overtaken by 'wuss' or 'wussy' but is still popular.

UK Influence

We haven't lost touch with the UK entirely however A few items of British English have also been going strong.

aggro
> aggressive, as in 'Don't be so aggro'. Our use is slightly different from the British one — we don't really talk about giving people aggro.

bonk
> this has become a half-joking, half-euphemistic word for having sex.

naff off
> Princess Anne told some journalists to 'naff off' once and has never been allowed to forget it

New Right
> Australian politics on the Liberal side has been ruled by the New Right but what made Mrs Thatcher a force to be reckoned with in British politics has not been a great success in Australian politics. We have picked up the jargon — the Liberal party here has been divided into wets and drys, and the wets have mostly left politics.

minder
> the television program *Minder* was very popular so a few expressions have drifted through from that. The word 'minder' no longer applies to a crook's bodyguard, but to anyone whose job it is to shield someone else from all kinds of unpleasantness. Pop stars have minders, as do politicians.

Aboriginal Influence

There are not a huge number of words in Australian English that are borrowed from Aboriginal languages (in fact, about 440) but they flavour the language in that they are significant cultural items. The pattern of borrowing is fairly straightforward and follows the pattern of European settlement in Australia. Captain Cook set the precedent with kangaroo. To European eyes this was an extraordinary animal and quite unlike anything they'd ever come across. So while there were many plants and animals that could be named a native this or that – the koala was originally called a native bear and the angophora was called the native apple – this creature could not be thought of as a native anything. So Captain Cook asked the Aborigines what they called it. These were Aborigines of North Queensland, of the Guugu Yimidhirr tribe, since by sheer circumstance Cook had not actually seen any kangaroos in Australia until the Endeavour put in to repair the large hole made in it by the Great Barrier Reef. The Aborigines told him what they called the animal, he noted it in his diary, and thus the first major borrowing into Australian English came about.

There is a curious sequel to this story. Relations between Aborigines and Europeans in Australia went from bad to worse, so that after that first great influx of Aboriginal words in the colonial period of our history there was then no traffic between Aboriginal languages and Australian English. What was worse was that there was little record of Aboriginal languages kept, so that when people finally became interested enough to attempt to track down the origin of kangaroo, they couldn't find the word for kangaroo in the local language. They were possibly thrown off by the fact that whereas in English the difference between the **k** consonant and the **g** consonant is significant, in the language of the Guugu Yimidhirr there was seen to be no difference at all. While this was being sorted out, the folklore theory developed that in fact Cook had been hoodwinked by the Aborigines and that the word kangaroo meant 'I don't know'. Alternatively it meant something very rude. The misunderstanding has been sorted out   kangaroo means kangaroo in anyone's language, but the folklore still persists.

Borrowings into Australian English have been made from a number of different Aboriginal languages, depending on where the Europeans turned up, the largest number of borrowings being from languages of the eastern coast. They are mostly names of animals and plants.

The Sydney Region

bogie	swimming hole
bombora	a current over a submerged reef
boobook	a small owl or mopoke
boomerang	curved piece of wood used as a missile
bettong	a rat-kangaroo
corella	a large parrot, predominantly white with pink or orange-red markings
corroboree	an Aboriginal ceremony
currawong	a large black and white bird with yellow eyes and a loud ringing call
dingo	a native dog
geebung	a small tree
gibber	a rock or stone
gin	an Aboriginal woman
gunyah	a rough shelter or dwelling

koala	the marsupial
kurrajong	a tree
myall	wild, from an Aboriginal word meaning 'stranger'
nulla-nulla	Aboriginal club or weapon
pademelon	a wallaby
potoroo	a small wallaby
wallaby	a small kangaroo
waratah	a flower with large showy red flowers, the emblem of New South Wales
warrigal	a dingo
wombat	a marsupial of the size of a large pig which lives in a burrow and is nocturnal
woomera	an Aboriginal weapon

Southern Victoria

bingie	the stomach or belly
belah	a tree
yabba	to talk
luderick	a fish

Tasmania

lubra	an Aboriginal woman

Southern South Australia

willy-willy	a sudden circling gust of wind
wurley	a rough shelter
joey	the young of the kangaroo

The Perth Region

euro	a wallaby
kylie	a boomerang
quokka	a small wallaby
wongi	to talk
bardy	an edible grub
karri	a eucalypt
jarrah	a large eucalypt
marron	a crayfish
wandoo	a eucalypt

Inland Victoria

mallee	a tree
mia-mia	a rough shelter
mulga	a type of wattle

Inland New South Wales

billabong	a waterhole
brigalow	a tree
coolamon	a wooden dish
gidgee	a tree
yarraman	a horse
brolga	a bird
quandong	a tree with an edible fruit
budgerigar	a small brightly coloured bird

The Brisbane Region

barramundi	a fish
dilly	a bag made of twisted grass or fibre
yakka	work

North Queensland

cooee	a cry made to signal one's presence in the bush
kangaroo	the kangaroo

The Outback

coolabah	a tree
nardoo	a fern

Recent Times

In the last ten years or so there has been another shifting in the status of Aboriginal languages and of Australian English, with the result that after decades of no borrowings at all we now have some new additions. A notable one is Koori, a word from the Awakabal tribe near Newcastle, just north of Sydney. Koori has been used by some Aborigines to refer to an Aborigine of eastern Australia since the early part of this century.

This shift in attitude is also noticeable in place names, beginning with the reinstating of the Loritdja word for that great red monolith in Central Australia, Uluru, formerly known as Ayers Rock. Similarly the Olgas are now the Kata Tjuta, as they have been known for a very long while apart from the small period of European settlement.

The following are some placenames that have been anglicised along with their meaning:

Allora	'waterhole'; a town in Queensland
Amaroo	'beautiful place' or 'red mud' or 'rain'; a town in NSW
Babinda	'waterfall'; a town in Queensland
Dandenong	'lofty mountain'; a mountain range in Victoria
Dorrigo	'stringybark'; a town in NSW
Dunedoo	'swan'; a town in NSW
Ekibin	a part of the river where Aborigines obtained edible aquatic roots; a locality in Brisbane
Murrumbidgee	'big water'; a river in NSW
Narooma	'blue water'; a town in NSW
Wagga Wagga	'crows'; a town in NSW
Waikerie	'wings or anything that flies'; a town in South Australia
Ulladulla	'safe harbour'; a coastal town in NSW

Sometimes these anglicised names and meanings originate from Aboriginal legends; legends which have been taken aboard by English speakers:

Arkaroolaa
> town in the northern Flinders Range in South Australia. (The place of Arkaroo, a great legendary Dreamtime snake which drank Lake Frome dry and carved out the bed of the Arkoola Creek and then filled it by passing water.)

Gidgealpaa
> town in South Australia. (To stand in the shade of a grey rain cloud, a reference to Kilyalpani, one of the mythical women who created the land. She once prayed for rain and while she was praying a grey cloud formed above her.)

Aboriginal Myths

Whatever the successes and failures of Aboriginal words in Australian English, a small set of them are entrenched in the national folklore. What would Australia be without the bunyip, that mythical creature who lives in the waterhole, is thought to cause loud noises at night and to devour women and children? The bunyip comes to us from Wemba-Wemba, a language of western Victoria, and was first reported in the *Port Philip Herald* in 1847. An interesting description appears in the same year in *Bell's Life in Sydney* 19 June. 'That apocryphal animal of many names, commonly designated "The Bunyip" has, according to a correspondent of the *Sydney Morning Herald*, been seen on the Murrumbidgee. It is described as being about as big as a six months old calf, of dark brown colour, a long neck, a long pointed head, large ears, a thick mane of hair from the head down the neck, and two large tusks. It is said to be an amphibious animal, as it has been observed floundering in the rivers, as well as grazing on their banks.'

From Wemba-Wemba we also have the mindi, a mythical hairy snake, which also lies in wait at waterholes (waterholes seem to be, mythologically speaking, extremely dangerous places). There is also the yowie to watch out for (this one comes from the Yuwaalaraay of north New South Wales). The yowie is a huge ape-like monster, a kind of Australian bigfoot – the Aboriginal word translated as meaning 'dream spirit'. And finally beware the min-min light, a will-of-the-wisp which is regarded as an evil apparition and which turns up on the plains of northern Queensland.

Abbreviations

Abbreviations for the States & Territories

Australia consists of six states and two territories.

NSW	New South Wales
Vic	Victoria
Tas	Tasmania
SA	South Australia
WA	Western Australia
NT	Northern Territory
Qld	Queensland
ACT	Australian Capital Territory

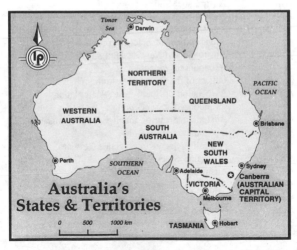

Australia's States & Territories

Acronyms & Abbreviations

7-Eleven	convenience store
AAP	Australian Associated Press
AAT	Australian Antarctic Territory
ABC	Australian Broadcasting Corporation
AC	Companion of the Order of Australia
ACTU	Australian Council of Trade Unions
ACF	Australian Conservation Foundation
AFI	Australian Film Institute
AFL	Australian Football League
ALP	Australian Labor Party
AM	Member of the Order of Australia
AMA	Australian Medical Association
AMF	Australian Military Forces
ANU	Australian National University (Canberra)
ANZAAS	Australian and New Zealand Association for the Advancement of Science (pronounced *an-zas*)
Anzac	Australian and New Zealand Army Corps (pronounced *an-zak*)
AO	Officer of the Order of Australia
ASEAN	Association of South-East Asian Nations (pronounced *ay-zee-an*)
ASIO	Australian Security Intelligence Organisation (pronounced *ay-zee-oh*)
ASIS	Australian Secret Intelligence Service
ASX	Australian Stock Exchange
ATC	Australian Tourist Commission
ATO	Australian Taxation Office
BASS	Ticket office for major entertainment events
BCA	Business Council of Australia
BYO(G)	Bring your own (grog). Some restaurants are only licensed for patrons to bring wine, etc with them.

CAA	Community Aid Abroad (Australian Oxfam)
CES	Commonwealth Employment Service. Offices around the country give advice for job seekers.
CHOGM	Commonwealth Heads of Government Meeting (pronounced *chog-um.*)
COAG	Council of Australian Governments *(ko-ag)*
CofE	Church of England
CPI	Consumer Price Index
CSIRO	Commonwealth Scientific & Industrial Research Organisation
CST	Central Standard Time (South Australia & the Northern Territory – 9.5 hours ahead of GMT/UTC)
CWA	Country Women's Association
DLP	Democratic Labor Party
EG	The *Entertainment Guide* in Friday's *Age* (newspaper). This is the one to read for info on what to do, see and listen to.
EPA	Environment Protection Authority
EST	Eastern Standard Time (10 hours ahead of Greenwich Mean Time. All eastern states are in this zone.)
GG	Governor-General
GPO	General Post Office
GST	Goods and Services Tax
HMAS	Her Majesty's Australian Ship
HR	House of Representatives
HSC	Higher School Certificate
LA	Legislative Assembly
M	(Films, TV) for mature audiences (15 years and over)
MCG	Melbourne Cricket Ground

MHA	Member of the House of Assembly
MHR	Member of the House of Representatives
MLA	Member of the Legislative Assembly
MLC	Member of the Legislative Council
MLG	Member of Local Government
MP	Member of Parliament
MTC	Melbourne Theatre Company. The principal theatre company in Melbourne.
NGA	National Gallery of Australia
NGV	National Gallery of Victoria
NIDA	National Institute of Dramatic Art (pronounced *nee-dah)*
NRMA	National Roads & Motorists' Association (of New South Wales)
OAM	Medal of the Order of Australia
OM	Order of Merit
OYO	'own your own' apartment
PAYE	Pay as you earn
PG	(Films, TV) parental guidance (recommended for children under 15)
PIN	Personal Identification Number
R	(Films, TV) unsuitable for people under the age of 18 years of age; stands for 'restricted exhibition'
RAAF	Royal Australian Air Force
RACV	Royal Automobile Club of Victoria. The equivalent of the AA in the UK and New Zealand.
RAN	Royal Australian Navy
RBA	Reserve Bank of Australia
RMIT	Royal Melbourne Institute of Technology
RRP	Recommended Retail Price
RSL	Returned Services League (of Australia)
RSPCA	Royal Society for the Prevention of Cruelty to Animals

RWC	Road Worthy Certificate. Obligatory saftey check before a car changes hands (Victoria)
SCG	Sydney Cricket Ground
SM	Stipendiary Magistrate
SBS	Special Broadcasting Service. TV and radio station focusing on multicultural programmes.
STA	State Transit Authority (NSW). Also international for Student Travel Australia.
STD	Subscriber Trunk Dialling. You need to use STD codes when dialling numbers outside local zones.
TAFE	Technical & Further Education (pronounced *tayf*)
TEC	Tertiary Education Commission
TPC	Trade Practices Commission
VAT	value added tax *(vat)*
VFA	Victorian Football Association
V/Line	interstate and country train services in Victoria
WEA	Workers' Educational Association
WRAAF	Women's Royal Australian Air Force
WRAN	Women's Royal Association Navy
WST	Western Standard Time (Western Australia – eight hours ahead of Greenwich Meantime)
YHA	Youth Hostels Association (now known worldwide as Hostelling International)
YMCA	Young Men's Christian Association
YWCA	Young Women's Christian Association

Food & Drink

In between Hullo and Goodbye there is eating and drinking, and the possibilities for this are endless. There is not yet anything which can be claimed as a national cuisine, although there are a few Australian specialties such as damper (bread cooked on an open fire) and floaters (meat pie floating in pea soup). What many Australians still have is an essentially British diet (meat, three veg, greens followed by pudding) which has adapted into an Australian environment. Thus in country cafés you can still have the mixed grill, which gives you any amount of meat (sausages, bacon, steak) with an Australian salad (a bit of lettuce, slice of tomato, tinned pineapple and beetroot). This is always served with bread and butter and washed down with tea or a kind of milky coffee. For dessert or pudding you can have lamingtons (slabs of sponge cake dipped in chocolate and coconut).

This kind of diet has been overtaken since WW II by the culinary

60

contributions of various migrant groups. Once we drank tea. Then thanks to the Italian community we tasted our first espresso coffees and cappuccinos. We are now so at home with these that you can find people ordering a 'cup of chino'. In the last couple of decades we have come to terms with the caffelatte, the macchiato, the short black, and much much more. Also since WW II was the advent of the BYO concept – the custom of patrons bringing wine or beer with them on a night out. This allowed ethnic cafés and small restaurants to flourish, as outlays were much lower for places with BYO licences compared with fully licensed places.

The national culinary consciousness has digested other major influences in recent years. Of worldwide significance was that which began with nouvelle cuisine, introduced to Australia in the early '80s. It was then superseded in the '90s by an eclectic international food based around a spicey, oriental cuisine with a European influence. With the ever-increasing cultural proximity of our Asian neighbours, the new restaurants of the '80s were Vietnamese, Thai, Korean and a second wave of Japanese, and these have become everyday styles of eating in the '90s.

European Australian tastes have shifted away from a colonial upbringing towards an international future.

Food in General

nosh

an old-fashioned word for food in general, as in 'Do you feel like some nosh?' In the past people have also eaten chow, grub, and tucker.

munchies

are snacks. Chips, pies, chocolate bars, and so on would be classed as munchies. To have an attack of the munchies is to suffer sudden severe pangs of hunger, a fate which befalls dope smokers in particular.

a spread

is a magnificent offering of food and drink, the veritable groaning board. A spread offers you the chance of a 'blow-out' or 'bean-feast', that is, an indulgence in food until your distended stomach can take no more. One result of this approach to eating is the popularity of the 'all-you-can-eat' restaurants, commonly found in the suburbs.

junk food

is a pretty general term for any kind of food which parents would disapprove of. Fried food, pizza, or a Mac attack fall into this category as do all kinds of lollies and chips. The fried food is also called 'greasies' which mostly refers to fish and chips but can be anything cooked in oil. Another general name for fast food is 'chew-an'-spew' — a rather jaundiced view perhaps.

Meals

Brekkie

consists of a cuppa (cup of tea) and a piece of toast with cocky's joy (treacle or golden syrup) or perhaps Vegemite (a vegetable extract), perhaps a goog or googey-egg (hen's egg), cereal and cow juice (milk)

Morning Tea

mostly bikkies and a cuppa with the occasional indulgence in a cake or bun

Brunch

breakfast and lunch combined, usually at weekends

Lunch

usually referred to as 'a bite of lunch', can vary in size depending on the occasion. Most commonly it is sangers (sandwiches).

Afternoon tea
 bring out the lamingtons, the Anzac biscuits, the carrot cake, the
 fly cemetery (fruit slice)
Dinner
 or 'din-dins'—this is serious stuff, the main meal of the day

Food You Might Encounter

bangers	sausages
barra	barramundi (a fish)
bubble & squeak	leftover vegetables, mashed and fried
bum-nuts	eggs
cackleberries	eggs
caulie	cauliflower
chockies	chocolates
chook	chicken
dagwood	very large sandwich
dead horse	sauce
dodger	bread
drumstick	chicken leg
flake	fillet of shark
hedgehog	chocolate-flavoured delicacy based on crushed Arrowroot biscuits
husband-beater	a long loaf of bread, a French loaf
marge	margarine
moo-juice	milk
muddie	Queensland mud crab
mushies	mushrooms
mystery bags	sausages

nana	banana
pav	pavlova (a traditional Australian meringue and cream dessert, named after the ballerina Anna Pavlova)
battered sav	saveloy in batter
snag	sausage
spud	potato
strawbs	strawberries

Tradenames

There are some food items which have become such a part of the Australian way of life that we would starve to death without them.

Vegemite
not a chocolate spread but a yeast extract to be spread on toast or Sayo biscuits. Some people like their Vegemite spread thinly, others like it in little dabs, and others like it spread thickly — it depends on the level of addiction. A famous advertising jingle has given rise to the expression 'happy little Vegemites' (sometimes 'good little Vegemites') which refers to contented and well-behaved little children of the kind appearing in the ad and singing the jingle.

Coon cheese
a kind of basic cheddar cheese. Nothing to do with the 'coon' of American English.

Arnotts arrowroot biscuits
a plain sweet biscuit which is the starting point for a number of desserts or confections

Mild Thirst
How about whetting your whistle.
What about a drop, mate. (both of these are older generation)

Extreme Hunger
He's got hollow legs. (said of someone who is always hungry)
I could eat a horse.
My stomach thinks my throat's cut.
I've got the munchies. (used to be after dope but is now general)

Extreme Thirst
Your tongue's hanging out.
dry as a bone
dry as a pommy's towel

The Second Drink
I could go another one.
How about anotherie? (a trifle
quaint)
That one didn't touch the sides.

Ordering Drinks
While all Australians agree on drinking beer, the different states
have different ideas on how to go about doing it. Here is a short guide
to some of the terms related to beer drinking:

beer	means lager in Victoria – a 'pot of beer' gets you a glass of lager
bobby	in WA a 6 oz glass
butcher	in SA a 6 oz glass
Darwin stubbie	a very very large beer bottle
dead marine	an empty beer bottle

Sayo biscuits
   a large water biscuit, usually smothered in butter and vege
   or served with Coon cheese

Iced vo-vos
   a very popular sweet biscuit

Aeroplane jelly
   comes in pretty packets and now in a range of Australian
   vours such as 'lillypilly', Also has a very popular jingle — 'I
   Aeroplane jelly, Aeroplane jelly for me.'

Childrens' Party Food

soft drink	any non-alcoholic drink
lolly water	any aerated soft drink
cordial	any not aerated soft drink
little boys	cocktail frankfurts
cheerios	cocktail frankfurts
fairy bread	buttered bread with hundreds and thousands on it
fairy floss	known as candy floss in other countries, and to be found at fairs
lollies	confectionary, sweets

Hunger

Hunger can range from mild appetite to pangs of starvation and a
raging thirst. Aussies have expressions to cope with all these situations.

Mild Appetite
I wouldn't mind a bite.
How about a quick bite.

echo	in SA a small beer bottle
eighteen	an eighteen-gallon beer keg
glass	in WA a 5 oz glass
grog	general term for beer or spirits
handle	a medium-sized beer glass with a handle.
liquid amber	general term for beer. Also called 'slops' or 'suds'.
middy	in NSW a 10 oz glass. In WA a 7 oz glass.
nine	a nine-gallon beer keg
pot	in WA a 10 oz glass
schooner	in NSW a 15 oz glass. In SA a 9 oz glass.
stubbie	a small beer bottle
tinny	a tin of beer – also called a 'tube'

Wine has increased in popularity amongst Australian drinkers and Australian wines are getting a solid reputation around the world. Here are some of the terms related to wine drinking:

chateau cardboard	cask wine
plonk	cheap wine. Also called 'bombo', 'red ned' and 'steam'.
vino	general word for wine

Pubs, Clubs & RSLs

A pub can be anything from a small bush shanty with bar and verandah to a glossy city number, flash and fancy. If it is close to you and favoured by you then it is known as the local. It is also called the rubbidy (rhyming slang, rubbidy dub means pub) or the pisser. Most pubs have bottle shops to sell wine, beer, etc, to take away, but there are bottle shops which operate independently of pubs. There are also wine shops which specialise in wine.

The clubs are notably the football clubs which have associated football teams. Football used to cover Rugby League, Rugby Union, Australian Rules and Soccer, but the younger generation seem to use it for just the first three and insist that soccer is soccer, not football. Pointing out that soccer has more claim to the term football than any of the others cuts no ice.

The RSL is the Returned Soldiers' League. You may be asked to be silent for a minute in honour of our fallen soldiers. Otherwise it is indistinguishable from other clubs and is affectionately known as the 'Rozzer'.

The Aussie Party

The party (otherwise known as 'a bit of a bash' amongst older Australians) is central to the Australian expectation of having a good time in life.

These days, the average urban party-goer may well be spotted in the traditional place alongside the barbecue (especially if male) and wearing a T shirt and shorts. However, he or she may be knocking back the chilled chardonnay rather than the old-fashioned tinny, and conversation will focus on the latest arty film as often as the footy results. The time-honoured rituals described below survive mostly in conservative social groups.

First of all everyone drinks and talks — this is the warming up. In the old days the men talked to the men (about sport mainly) and the women talked to the women (about clothes and children). A few party games help to relax everyone — these can be as simple as chasing people to put ice down their necks or as complicated as a game of pool. The midnight swim is still a favourite — on the beach or in the pool. At some stage in the evening the boys will become *the boys* and do silly things — throw rocks on the roof of the neighbour's house to wake them up or attempt to drive the car onto the roof for a better view. They will also turn the music up very loud. The police will be called and possibly, in the most successful parties, the fire brigade. There's not much you can do with the police but the fire brigade has been known to pose for party pics. The women will take command and

69

hush and shush the boys until they promise to behave. Eventually they will collapse into sleep now that the high point of the party has been achieved.

• party	bit of a bash, shindig, rage, beano, wing-ding, piss-up, booze-up
• conversation	small talk, chit-chat, rap, bit of a yarn (especially amongst older men), gossip session, a wongi
• to chat	bat the breeze, chew the fat or rag, have a natter (older females, or men describing their way of talking)

Drinking Protocol

Go immediately to the bottle shop and buy whatever poison takes your fancy and that you think you can handle for the night. No — it's not a suggestion that suicide might be preferable to what follows. Poison is drink — alcoholic drink. Most commonly you will go to the party armed with tinnies (tins of beer) which you may purchase in a slab (a carton of 24 beer cans), or you may opt for the trusty cask of plonk (cheap wine, red or white). As soon as you get to the party it will be suggested that you have a rosiner — one to whet your whistle. Note that either verbally or in writing you will have been informed that the party is BYO (sometimes BYOG). This means that you Bring Your Own (Grog). Sometimes barbecues will be labelled BYOGM which means Bring Your Own Grog and Meat – the host will then provide the extras.

The Argument

Undoubtedly you will have a bit of a barney (old-fashioned word for argument) with someone, which usually sets out to be of the friendly good-humoured variety but which in some cases takes a serious turn. Most often the friendly arguments are about sport, even politics. There is a wide range of useful words you can apply to your opposition which are acceptable as long as the basic intention is amiable and they are uttered with a reassuring smile.

boofhead
    possibly derived from a 16th century word *buffle* for a fool, which was a borrowed French term of abuse (in French it meant 'buffalo')

you great galah
    galahs have a bad reputation in Australia for being noisy, gregarious, and stupid

dumbcluck
    this draws on the well-known idiocy of chickens

nincompoop
    someone has suggested that this is related to 'non compos' but no one really knows.

bloody drongo
    Drongo was a horse that insisted on coming second in all its races rather than first.

Temper

• lose one's temper	spit the dummy, blow a fuse, lose one's cool, blow one's stack or top, chuck a wobbly, cut up rough, do one's block or nana, flip one's lid, go off one's brain, go through the roof, go nuts or bonkers, chuck a mental, spit chips, get off one's bike
• argument	bit of a barney, bust-up, ding or wing-ding, set-to, argy-bargy
• angry	fit to be tied, foaming at the mouth, hot under the collar, mad as a cut snake, mad as a maggot, off one's face, ropeable
• cross with someone	dark on someone, dirty on someone, miffed shirty, snaky, sore, narked on someone

• in a bad mood	browned off, cheesed off, fed up to the back teeth, have the shits, pissed off, snitchy, uptight
• crazy	silly as a two-bob watch, not the full quid, has kangaroos in the top paddock, has gone troppo
• idiot	imbo (short for imbecile), a mug alec, a nerd, a dork
• to tease	chiack, razz someone, send them up, take the mickey out of them, stir
• to abuse	bore it up someone, get stuck into someone, give someone a blast, give them heaps, tip the bucket on them
• a fight	a blue, a box-on, a bust-up, barney, dust-up, go-in, a rough-house, set-to, donnybrook, free-for-all, punch-up, run-in, yike
• to fight	to mix it with someone, come to blows, go the knuckle, stack on a turn, bash up
• back off, get scared	go to water, pack shit, pack death, take a willy, chicken out, pike out, show the white feather
• coward	a gutless wonder, a damp squib, cowardy custard, dingo, nervous Nellie, scaredy-cat, sook, wimp, yellow-belly, piker, poofter
• be in trouble	the shit hits the fan, be in more strife than Ned Kelly (Australian bushranger hanged in 1880), be up shit creek in a barbed wire canoe without a paddle.
• 'get stuffed!'	Get a rat up ya! Get a big black dog up ya!

The 'Good Guys'

fair dinkum

this expression comes from Lancashire dialect and refers to the basic notion that a fair day's work (or dinkum) demands a fair day's pay. There is a story that dinkum is a Chinese word meaning 'real gold' and refers to the anxieties of the goldfields when distinguishing real from false gold was an issue, but this is folklore.

good sport
> people, men or women, who have never played sport let along a team sport in their lives can still be described as good sports. It is one of the highest accolades. A good sport is good-natured and uncomplaining, accepts chiacking cheerfully, and is willing to give something or someone a go.

tall poppie
> an achiever. Knockers (critics) will always want to cut them down.

Fair Dealing

• deal honestly	play it straight, play with a straight bat, play fair, lay it on the line
• truth	the good oil, the drum, the full two bob, the good guts, the griff, the real thing, the straight wire
• honest person	plain-dealer, square-shooter, straight talker
• honest	up-front, aboveboard, dinky-di, ridgy-didge, straight up and down

The 'Bad Guys'

Amongst the guests at the party will be the inevitable bullshit artist, the con man who wants to confide to you his latest lurk or rort. To rort the system is to twist the rules or procedures of an organisation in a manner which is either illegal or bordering on illegality for one's own advantage. This used to be an activity popularly thought to be a political speciality but has spread now that we all realise it is quite a good idea. Rorts are also known as scams or shonks.

bludger
> a person who lives off other people, either financially
> or emotionally

cadger
> like a bludger, a bloodsucker, parasite

yobbos
> bad guys might just be yobbos (or yobs), that is, uncouth,
> aggressive people with no subtlety to their antisocial
> behaviour

dobber
> a person who reports a scam, rort, bludger, etc

- cadge   put the bite on, put the fangs into, bot, bludge, fang, put the hard word on, sting, touch, put the nips into
- scheme   rort, scam, shonk, dodge, hum, sting, touch

The Food

Congratulatory remarks to the host
or hostess go along the following
lines:

It's grouse.
It's great nosh.

Say cheerfully to the provider 'you're a terrific bloke/sheila and your blood's worth bottling' and watch his/her face light up with pleasure. Then with a cry of 'Bog in, don't wait' you can leap on the food.

If on the other hand the food is terrible you can mutter to your neighbour that it would kill a brown dog.

Inebriation

- drunk   high as a kite, blotto, tanked, sloshed, plastered, drunk as Chloe (a nude in a painting hanging on the wall of a bar in Melbourne), full as a goog, tight as a tick, pissed as a newt/parrot/fart, mollo, pissed out of one's brain, pissed to the eyeballs, primed, shickered, sozzled, stewed to the gills, tanked

- drugged   off the planet, off one's face, high, stoned, bombed, loaded, ripped, smashed, stoked, spaced out, spacey

- throw up   chunder, spew, drive the porcelain bus

Departure

If you have any brains still operational you should at this point leave. Cheerio, you say, I'm going to chuff off now. I'm going to shoot through like a Bondi tram, chuck it in for the night, tie a knot in my bluey.

If your brains are not operational, stay and have another drink. And so we move to that point in the evening when someone suggests that you could get a great view of the Opera House by driving the car up onto the roof. On with the police and the fire brigade and the ultimate collapse.

PS. You probably won't want to talk to anyone the next day but just supposing you could talk you might admit to a hangover with symptoms described as the horrors, the Joe Blakes (shakes), the DTs, blue devils, pink elephants and dingbats. You would deny however that you are a heavy drinker. You are most certainly not:

an alkie
a booze artist
a grog artist
a hard case
a lush (if you're a woman)
a pisspot

No indeed, you say, usually I'm a two-pot screamer (totally off your head after just two drinks of beer). What happened last night is an aberration, a dreadful mistake, a case of keeping bad company, a never-to-be-repeated fiasco. Never? Well, not till next time, anyhow.

City & Bush

The basic division, physically and culturally, for many Australians is the city and the bush.

Most Australians live in the cities which are all, with the exception of Canberra, on the coastal fringe. As a city Canberra is a deliberate creation and upsets the natural order of things anyhow. But because we mostly live in the city, we tend to dream about the bush – its stands of trees, its vast plains, its mountain ranges, its rivers and inland seas. It has achieved mythical status and is inhabited by heroes of folklore and activated by fictionalised events.

Country Places

There are various mythical places in this mental map of the bush.

Bullamakanka
> an imaginary remote town. It has a pseudo-Aboriginal name and is totally hicksville. It is also called 'Woop-Woop', or 'Bandy-wallop'.

back of Bourke
> a vague and unspecified area which is beyond Bourke, a remote town in north-western NSW, on the fringe of the outback. Woop-Woop and Bullamakanka are probably back of Bourke.

beyond the black stump
> there are a million pubs and motels in NSW which will claim to have the authentic black stump that people went beyond. Do not believe them. The phrase appears to have come from the practice of giving directions in regions where

77

landmarks are strange-shaped rocks, identifiable hills, and the ubiquitous blackened stump. The blackened stump became the last known point of civilisation. If you went beyond that you were on your own.

the never-never

remote outback regions, more precisely areas of Queensland and the Northern Territory. There is a theory that the term is an anglicisation of an Aboriginal name for the same region, Nivah Nivah, but the English version conjures up the ultimate state of being lost and forgotten.

Identifiable Regions

There are regions which are identified by vegetation.

the mallee

this can apply to a number of semi-arid areas in NSW, SA, and WA, but in particular to a region in Victoria where the mallee grows. The mallee is a species of eucalypt but it appears to have no trunk at all, the branches rising straight from the ground. What it does have is an enormous and tough root system, a fact that broke the hearts of many farmers who tried to dig it out. Mallee root makes good firewood though.

the brigalow

is a kind of acacia or wattle. It is not an unpleasant tree but it is difficult to clear for farming because of its habit of suckering. The cattle tend to get lost in it too and will only eat the foliage when they are very hard up. One way or another it hampers operations and can cause brigalow itch, a form of dermatitis.

the saltbush

sheep will eat saltbush but then it only grows in semi-desert and salty regions of central Australia where nothing else grows anyway.

the scrub

scrub is land covered by shrubby bushes, often thickly growing to the point where it is bordering on impenetrable, and indicating poor soil. To be out in the scrub or the scrubs is to be where no one else particularly wants to join you. It is not only remote but it is impoverished and unpleasant.

the spinifex

spinifex is a spiny grass of a genus which is mostly found in arid zones of Australia. It is a tussocky kind of grass which puts its own stamp on the outback regions where it grows.

Europeans & the Bush

The bush of our collective memory has the whitening bones of explorers, the cries of 'Bail up!' from the bushrangers, the farmers ranging from the cocky farmers to the bunyip aristocracy, the bushmen and the swaggies.

The Explorers

In the Australian way, the European explorers who live on in popular imagination are not the plodding and orthodox types like Sir Thomas Mitchell, a worthy surveyor and Government man who did a lot of good work in New South Wales and Victoria. The people we remember are the glorious failures. Take Burke and Wills, the pair who set out from Victoria to cross the continent in 1860. Robert O'Hara Burke was a dashing character whose impetuous decision to crash or crash through led to the death of the entire expedition. Ludwig Leichhardt was a German who arrived in Sydney in 1842 and was considered somewhat eccentric by conservative Sydney (Sir Thomas Mitchell for example did not take to him at all). But after one successful and one dismal expedition, he set out into the interior with a small party and was never seen again. This foray inspired Patrick White's novel *Voss*.

The Bushrangers

Bushranging begins and ends with Ned (Edward) Kelly (1855-80) who led the troopers a merry dance until he was finally caught and hanged in Melbourne Gaol. There are a lot of elements in the story which have led to Ned's becoming a kind of Robin Hood figure in Australian folklore, but the story of his capture is unique. Ned and his gang (mostly his brothers) had held up the entire town of Glenrowan in Victoria. Meanwhile the Melbourne establishment had sent out a train of police and trackers. Ned organised fettlers (railway workers) to dig up the tracks and derail the train, but the Glenrowan schoolmaster escaped and managed to stop the train in time. The bushrangers realised their plan had failed and donned homemade armour made from the metal of ploughs for the final shootout. But despite the armour the bushrangers were outnumbered. Ned's last words before he was hanged were said to be 'Such is life!'

There are a couple of other bushrangers who are worth a mention. Captain Moonlight and Captain Thunderbolt were good bushmen and rather elegant performers. Brave Ben Hall was in the more sinned against than sinning category – he took to bushranging because of basic injustice. Mad Dog Morgan on the other hand was noted for his brutality.

The Farmers

These fall into different categories:

cocky farmer
> is a small landholder — the idea is this kind of farmer resembles the cockatoo who scratches in the dirt to find a living. A cocky can be a cane cocky (sugar farming), a cow cocky (dairy farming) or a wheat cocky (wheat farming).

grazier
> is a station-owner and runs sheep or cattle. The grazier is the big landowner and much more likely to be part of the bunyip aristocracy or squattocracy (the *crème de la crème* of the bush).

jackeroo
> was a young man sent out to gain experience on a station, usually as a preliminary to running one of his own. The word is borrowed from an Aboriginal word, taken to mean 'wandering white man'. After the jackeroo came the 'jillaroo' — the female counterpart.

shearer
> is the man celebrated in the song 'Click Go the Shears Boys'.

> 'The ringer looks around and is beaten by a blow,
> And curses the old swaggie with the bare-belly yeo.'

Shearing has its own jargon – masses of it. The ringer is the fastest shearer in the shed, the one who runs rings around everyone else, but in this instance he is beaten by one blow, that is, one stroke of the shears. And what is worse he is beaten by an old swaggie, a nobody in the shearer's world. The reason the swaggie won is that he has a bare-belly yeo or ewe, a sheep that has defective wool growth that makes the wool come off easily.

rouseabout
> the station hand who is expected to do all the odd jobs. In the shearing shed he is the one who rushes up with the tar for a cut sheep and who gathers up the fleeces and takes them to the sorting table.

boundary rider

while every station has its fences which can cover vast acreage and which need to be regularly maintained, there have been incredibly long fences erected by State Governments for various reasons: to keep rabbits from crossing from eastern Australia to Western Australia or to keep dingoes out of settled NSW. Boundary riders patrolled these fences, often not seeing another human being for months on end. There is a tradition of boundary riders who are loners by nature and self-educated men, happy to be by themselves in the bush and armed with the complete works of Shakespeare in their saddlebag.

The bushman

or 'bushie' is the man who lives in the bush. The idea of the bushman is that he is totally at home in it and knows all its ways, he is never lost and never starves or dies of thirst, and he is usually on good terms with the Aborigines from whom he has learnt a thing or two.

The swagman

or 'swaggie' is the man who carries his swag on the wallaby track (shortened to 'on the wallaby'). Often a good bushman too. The sundowner is the swaggie who times his arrival at a station (sheep or cattle station) at about sundown, too late to be asked to do any work in return for his tea and sugar and flour.

The City

The city is referred to by bushies as the big smoke and its inhabitants are city slickers. City people are fast and dishonest and generally too clever by half. The bushie's only way of handling the city slicker is to be bold, upstanding, and belt him one.

The city/bush division still lives on in the country, but Australian cities have changed a lot in the last decade or so and are rather less concerned with the country and more concerned with either themselves (there is a lot of city introspection) or with the outside world, particularly the USA.

city

an important and confusing term in Australian English with various meanings. The city refers to either the whole of Sydney for example or to just the central part of it. There is a basic distinction between a city which is very big and a town which can be big or small but which is less important than a city. In the country the city can either be the city or the whole area surrounding it. You can be driving through the middle of nowhere and find a sign which tells you that you are now in the City of Bullamakanka. You look earnestly for a sign of civilisation and find none. Eventually you will find Bullamakanka itself but be prepared to drive for a while.

the suburbs

have been an object of derision – boring, dreary, etc, but are beginning to be discovered as having a life of their own

bungalow

the Californian bungalow is one of the basic housing styles of the Australian suburb. This basic architectural style imported from the goldfields of California in the 1850s has been adapted to Australian conditions perhaps more satisfactorily than any other. It is typically one storey with a buttress-like stone or pebble chimney, a deep verandah, and a simple, low-pitched spreading gabled tiled roof.

flat

the basic term for a place you rent as opposed to a place you own. Generally in an apartment building or divided house.

home unit

a division of a housing block which has a number of such dwellings in it. Shortened to 'unit'. It can be rented too.

apartment

not so common but definitely an up-market flat. A 'studio apartment' is a small flat which has something which makes it more interesting than just an ordinary flat, like a bay window or a skylight – something. A real estate agent's term.

granny flat

what used to be called in depression days a 'sleep-out'. What is quaintly called in Tasmania a 'chalet'. A small building out the back which can be used as a separate dwelling.

terrace house

Paddington terrace houses (Sydney) are famous because of the charm of the wrought iron on their balconies and because of the wealth of their owners. However terrace houses are common enough. They were basically last century's cheap housing for the poor, but since the war have become trendy housing for inner city dwellers.

villa
> a classier kind of modern terrace, slightly bigger than the model and with better bathrooms and kitchens.

duplex
> a two-storey block of flats or home units, each dwelling occupying one floor.

condo
> a condominium or large apartment. There are not many of these in Sydney. In Melbourne they tend to have sale prices of over a million.

semi-detached
> one of a pair of houses joined by a common wall.

cluster house
> one of a group of houses which share a block of land. A space-saver in suburbia where urban consolidation is the catchcry.

facadism
> the practice of retaining the façade of an old building while constructing a new one behind it.

inner city
> anywhere within walking distance of the main post office.

inner suburbs
> the ring of suburbs just beyond the inner city, that is, about seven km from the GPO. In Sydney the concept of the inner city is complicated by such facts as that most people do not consider North Sydney for example to be inner city. Once you cross the bridge (or go through the tunnel) you are on the North Shore which is a world unto itself. The inner city is a trendy place to live — café societies, yuppiedom, etc.

outer suburbs
> beyond the ring of the inner city are the outer suburbs. Essentially hicksville. In Sydney 'westies' live in the outer suburbs. Westies are considered by inner city folk to be uncool, dorks, nerds, etc. They are, in lifestyle, the antithesis of both the surfies who live on the beaches and the rad city dudes.

Australian
Aboriginal
Languages

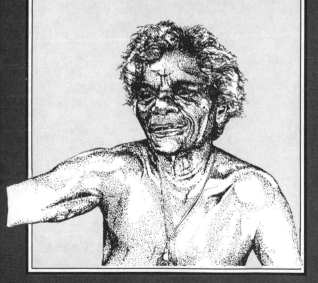

Introduction

The original inhabitants of Australia have been living on this continent for tens of thousands of years. When the British established the first European settlement in Australia at Port Jackson (Sydney) in 1788, the newcomers originally called the older inhabitants 'natives' and then 'Aborigines'. The latter term is in general use, but some Aboriginal people prefer one of their own names rather than 'Aborigine', which can be applied to any indigenous people. There is no self-designation that covers all Aboriginal people; the term Murri is used in Queensland, Nyoongah or Noongar in the southwest of Western Australia, Yolngu in northeastern Arnhem Land and Koori or Koorie in New South Wales and Victoria.

The size of the Aboriginal population at the time the first Europeans came to Australia is not known, but estimates run from a low 300,000 to over a million. The people were hunter-gatherers, that is they lived by hunting animals and gathering various plant foods. Each person belonged to a land-owning group, typically a clan with its own distinctive speech. Often a group of neighbouring clans would have similar forms of speech and we could say that these clans spoke dialects of a particular language.

It is now extremely difficult to ascertain the number of languages spoken prior to contact the Europeans, especially in areas where the Aboriginal population was wiped out and records of languages spoken are few. But it is clear that there were a great number of languages spoken throughout the land. In 1788 there were about 250 different languages in Australia, each comprising several dialects. However, over the course of the next hundred years the British took over the whole of Australia and in the process many Aboriginal people died, either as a result

of introduced diseases or through being shot or poisoned. In areas where fertile land attracted a denser pattern of European settlement, most of the Aboriginal population perished.

Today there are no speakers left of the languages of Tasmania, Victoria, and most of New South Wales. The only flourishing languages are to be found in the centre of the continent and along the north coast.

Relatedness

There is no clear connection between the languages of the mainland and those of Tasmania. Nor, indeed, is there a known connection between the languages of the mainland and Tasmania and any languages spoken elsewhere.

On the mainland, one way of classifying the languages is by distinguishing between Pama-Nyungan and non-Pama-Nyungan language families. The Pama-Nyungan is a very large group both in terms of numbers and the area the languages cover. The word Pama-Nyungan was made up out of the name for 'man, person' from the most north-easterly representative and the most south-westerly representative of this large language family. The Pama-Nyungan languages were spoken over the majority of the mainland, and as related languages they have a percentage of shared vocabulary, language structure and sounds that indicates a possible shared predecessor language. However the languages vary widely. There is no great similarity between *pama* and *nyunga,* just as there are few overt similarities between such related languages as English, Russian and Hindi.

The languages known as the non-Pama-Nyungan group are located to the north (the Top End) and the north-west (Kimberleys) of the mainland. The relationships between the various languages of this group are as yet unclear.

Sounds

There is some similarity amongst the Aboriginal languages with some of the sounds they use and the way these sounds are strung together. All the languages have the **ng** sound as in 'sing' and it is common for this sound to appear at the beginning of a word. The word for 'I', for instance, is often *ngaya* or something similar. Other common sounds are **ny** as in *bunya*, the Yagara name of a tall pine-like tree found in south-eastern Queensland, and r-coloured sounds such as **rd** in *nardoo*, a kind of flour made from the spores of various ferns. This word is actually *ngardu* and comes from the languages of western New South Wales and neighbouring states. Certain sounds found in English do not occur, such as the sibilants **s** (as in 'sack') and **sh** (as in 'shack').

In Aboriginal languages there is normally no distinction between members of the following pairs: **p** & **b**, **t** & **d**, **k** & **g**, and **ch** (also spelled **ty** or **tj**) & **j** (also spelled **dy** or **dj**). This is part of the reason that the names of some groups and their languages are variously spelled, such as Arunta/Aranda, nowadays Arrernte (central Australia), and Walbiri/Warlpiri (central Australia). Alternation between the members of these pairs can be a problem when it comes to using reference books, particularly where the alternation is in the initial consonant. The name of the original inhabitants of the Adelaide area, for instance, is spelled both Kaurna and Gaurna.

Here are a few more distinctive features of the sound systems of Aboriginal languages:

- There are a lot of nasal sounds – sounds made by letting the air pass through your nose, a bit like **m**, **n** and **ng** in English. There is also a retroflex (bent back) or 'r-coloured' **n** (**rn**), and a tongue-tip bent down of 'y-coloured' **n** (**ny**).
- There are retroflex (bent back) or 'r-coloured' sounds – made by holding the tongue tip curled back as for an English r while making such sounds as **t**, **n** and **l**. These sounds are often written with an **r**, eg **rt**, **rn**, **rl**, or in some languages with an underline eg **t̲**, **n̲**.

- There are tongue-tip bent down or 'y-coloured' sounds – made by holding the tongue tip down behind the lower front teeth while making such sounds as **t**, **n** and **l**. These sounds are often written with a **y**, eg **ty**, **ny** and **ly**
- Aboriginal languages do not usually utilise sounds like **th**, **f/v**, **s/z**, **sh** and **h**

Since Aboriginal words often contain sounds and sound sequences unfamiliar to speakers of English, they have often been recorded with various degrees of accuracy. The inaccurate rendering of *ngardu* was mentioned above. This word is also found as *ardu* with the initial *ng* missed altogether. Inaccuracy accounts for some of the variation found in the spelling of language names and place names. There is a language of the Echuca area of northern Victoria that is usually spelled Yota-Yota. There is an alternative spelling Yorta-Yorta which is more accurate in that it picks up the r-coloured or retroflex **t**. This name, like many other language names, is based on the word for 'no'. Different groups often had distinctive words for 'no' and people would name their neighbours after their 'no' word.

There are also problems with conveying the sounds of Aboriginal words accurately because of the irregular relationship between sound and spelling in English. For instance, in English the letter **u** represents one sound in 'but' and another in 'put'. The language of the bayside areas around Melbourne was recorded as Bunwurung and Bunarong, which gives a poor guide to the pronunciation. It is also recorded as Boonoorong which gives a better guide to the pronunciation of the vowels, but Bunarong has been perpetuated as the name of a park and several streets, and is pronounced in a way that the bearers of that name would never recognise.

Vocabulary

It has been a mistaken belief that Aboriginal languages have only a few words. In fact, of course, like any language they have thousands. Many of these words do not correspond directly to English words, rather they cover a different classification of the natural world and express concepts particular to Aboriginal culture.

A striking feature of Aboriginal vocabulary is that the words found in one language are usually quite different from those found in neighbouring languages and elsewhere. This means that if you learn one Aboriginal language, you do not have much of a start for learning a second one. However, there is a core of a few words that is widespread. This core of words includes the following:

bina	ear	*jina*	foot
bula	two	*mara*	hand
jalayn	tongue	*mili*	eye
jarra	thigh		

Structure

Aboriginal languages characteristically used different endings, added to words, to mark relations between words in a sentence. In the Kalkadoon language of the Mount Isa area, for instance, an ending is used to mark a word as responsible for an action. In the following example the ending *-yu* is attached to the word *martu* 'mother'.

Mother grabs the dog.   *Martu-yu ngulurmayi thuku.*

Since the suffix *-yu* indicates that it is mother who grabs the dog rather than the dog who grabs mother, the word order can be varied to show different degrees of emphasis. One could have the following, for instance.

Mother grabs the dog.   *Ngulurmayi thuku martu-yu.*

Here are two more endings: *-piangu* meaning 'from' and *-kunha* meaning 'to'.

| The policeman goes from | *Kanimayintyirr ingka* |
| Darwin to Melbourne. | *Darwin-piangu Melbourne-kunha.* |

The word *kanimayintyirr* means 'policeman'. Literally it is 'the one who ties up'; *kanimayi* is 'tie up' and *-nytyirr* is a suffix like *-er* in English words such as *driver*. This is an interesting example of how the Kalkadoon people made up a new word for the new concept of policeman.

Across the north of the continent languages tend to have very complex verbs that seem more like sentences than single words. In Tiwi, the language of Bathurst and Melville Islands, for instance, the English sentence 'He sent them a message' can be expressed as a single word *yu-wuni-marri-wa-yangirri,* literally, 'he-them-with-words-sent'.

Developments

As in other parts of the world where European colonisation and accompanying social disruption has taken place, creole languages have arisen in northern Australia. Two wide-spread creoles, Broken and Kriol, are spoken by many Aboriginal people in the Torres Strait and in the Top End respectively.

The sound system and certain areas of vocabulary are heavily influenced by the traditional languages of the region. Although the vocabulary of both Broken and Kriol is largely of English origin, many of these words have changed in meaning to embody traditional concepts and distinctions. In English the word 'we' refers to the speaker and one or more other persons. Aboriginal languages usually have a number of different words for 'we' distinguishing whether 'we' covers two people or more than two and whether the addressee (you) is included. These distinctions are carried over into the creoles. In the Kriol of Roper River, for instance, *yunmi* means 'we' in the sense of 'you and I', *mintupala* means 'we two' (not including you) and there are a number of words for 'we' covering more than two people. These include *wi*, *melapat* and *mipala*.

Well over a hundred of the original 250 or so languages have died and only a few score will survive into the next century, including several varieties of Kriol. However, Aboriginal people all over Australia are showing a renewed interest in preserving what they can of their languages and in trying to restore them from materials recorded during past generations. In many parts of Australia the present generation of Aboriginal children is being taught the language that belongs to their particular area.

Central Australian Languages

Introduction

The languages in central Australia (or the Centre, as it is often referred to) are among the strongest surviving Aboriginal languages in the country, as their speakers have had a relatively short history of contact with non-Aboriginal people. Despite this, the effects of non-Aboriginal settlement have been dramatic. Before non-Aboriginal people began to settle in central Australia in the 1870s, it is thought that there were more than 38 main languages and dialects in the area. The establishment of pastoral properties, the Overland Telegraph Line, missions and reserves and later towns such as Alice Springs has had a huge impact on the original inhabitants of central Australia. It has meant that many language groups have moved, or have been moved, from their traditional country, resulting in language change and in some cases, language loss to the point of extinction. Of the original 38 main languages and dialects, about seven are now considered endangered, and four are considered extinct or nearly extinct.

The main surviving language groups in central Australia are the group of Arandic languages and dialects, dialects of the Western Desert language, dialects of Warlpiri (Ngarrkic languages) and Warumungu. These languages belong to the Pama-Nyungan family of languages (see the Introduction to Aboriginal Languages). Unlike the fertile land in the Top End of Australia, or along the east coast of the continent, the arid lands of central Australia can only support a limited number of people. As a result, single language groups are spread over vast areas of land. The Western Desert language for example is one of the most widely spread indigenous languages in the world, extending from central Australia to the Great Australian Bight and the Indian Ocean.

In Alice Springs, the Language Centre at the Institute for Aboriginal Development (IAD; PO Box 2531, Alice Springs, 0871) runs language and cross-culture programs for Aboriginal and non-Aboriginal people from Alice Springs, as well as interstate and international visitors. The Institute also carries out research into central Australian languages, and produces dictionaries and other language-related publications of a high quality. In Tennant Creek, Papulu Apparr-kari, the Barkly Region Aboriginal Language Centre (PO Box 1108, Tennant Creek, 0861) coordinates language and culture programs for the Barkly region.

There are several bilingual schools in the central Australian region, where Aboriginal children learn in both their own language and in English. Most of these schools are in Aboriginal communities, apart from Yipirinya School, an independent school in Alice Springs. Aboriginal people can study their own languages, or prepare for careers in interpreting and translating, language teaching or dictionary work by attending courses run by the IAD or Batchelor College, an Aboriginal college based at Batchelor (south of Darwin) that has campuses in both Alice Springs and Tennant Creek.

Talking with Aboriginal People

Some Aboriginal people in central Australia speak standard Australian English. Others, especially those who speak another language as their first language, may use a different kind of English, often known as Aboriginal English. Aboriginal English uses mostly English words, but takes its grammar, sounds and most of its cultural meanings from Aboriginal languages.

Many travellers would be aware of how insulting it is to be spoken to in 'pidgin' by a fluent speaker of a language. Or of how frustrating it is when someone speaks to you in a loud voice — as if you were deaf, rather than unable to understand the language. It is important to remember this when speaking to people who do not speak

Many language speakers are bilingual or multilingual, speaking one or more Aboriginal languages or dialects as well as English. Although languages in the Centre share a few common characteristics, they are for the most part very different from each other.

The names of languages and dialects used in central Australia have become quite widely known. Often, they describe where the people who speak that language come from, or describe a feature of their language which distinguishes it from another language nearby:

Ikngerre-ipenhe Arrernte	eastern Arrernte
Pitjantjatjara	having the word *pitja* (come).

Keeping Languages Strong

Apart from speaking their languages to their children and grandchildren, Aboriginal people are working hard in language centres, schools and media outlets to ensure that their languages survive.

In Alice Springs, the Central Australian Aboriginal Media Association (CAAMA) broadcasts programs in English and in local languages on 100.5 FM. Also in Alice Springs, Imparja Television broadcasts occasional programs in Aboriginal languages with English subtitles (for example, *Nganampa Anwernekenhe* — check local newspapers for program details). There are a number of bands playing contemporary and more traditional Aboriginal music, including songs in Aboriginal languages, around the Centre. The CAAMA Shop (see details below under References) stocks cassette tapes, compact discs and some videos of local Aboriginal bands.

English as their first language. Speak slowly and clearly, but don't insult people by using baby talk or a kind of pidgin language, and don't speak in a voice that is louder than your normal speaking voice.

Asking direct questions (especially 'why' questions such as 'Why aren't you coming?') is considered rude by many Aboriginal people. It is better to make suggestions or to talk around the issue, than to ask direct questions. Don't always expect exact replies to your questions either. It is unlikely that you will be given anything but the most public information by people that you have just met. Don't embarrass people by asking questions about anything that could be considered private, or expect that people have got the time to stop and answer all of your questions. Many Aboriginal people are tired of being harassed by non-Aboriginal people on a search for spiritual or cultural knowledge, but may be too polite to say so. If you are particularly interested in finding out more about Aboriginal culture and spirituality, you may want to join a tour organised by Aboriginal people (see Travelling & Staying on Aboriginal Land in this chapter), or enrol in a language or cross-culture course organised by the Institute for Aboriginal Development or Papulu Apparr-kari.

Central Australian languages, like most Australian languages do not have words for greetings like 'hello'. Aboriginal people are now accustomed to English speakers using greetings, and some languages have adopted greetings based on the English form. These are used mainly to greet non-Aboriginal people, especially those who have begun to learn the language. Language speakers do not use these greetings when talking to each other. Instead, they often call out a person's 'skin' name or use a relationship term (see Family Relationships, pages 101-102).

Likewise, central Australian languages don't have words for 'please' or 'thank you'.

Although these days, more and more people use the English 'thank you', thanks is sometimes still expressed in actions rather than words. If someone does something for you, you can show your thanks by doing something for that person at a later date. Similarly, if someone gives you something, it would be appropriate to reciprocate by giving them something in return at another time. Money may be given, or material goods, knowledge, or even friendship in exchange.

It is not polite to ask people 'What is your name?', as many English speakers may do to start a conversation. If you want to know a person's name, it is better to ask another person nearby 'What is that person's name?'. A better way of starting a conversation is to refer to a recent local event, or perhaps to admire a child who is with the person you are speaking with. Another way is to tell them where you are from, and ask them where they are from.

Among Aboriginal language speaking adults, first names are used much less than in non-Aboriginal society. People tend to use relationship terms, such as 'uncle' or 'daughter' when talking to each other. Some language groups, such as Warlpiri and Arrernte refer to each other by 'skin' names.

Many Aboriginal people use hand signs and gestures during everyday conversation and during ceremonies. These signs are not limited to the deaf community, but are used and understood by all language speakers. As you walk around Alice Springs, you may be aware of people using handsigns to communicate with each other across long distances, like across the Todd River or busy roads, or in other situations where talking or shouting is not practical.

Aboriginal people do not use eye contact as much as non-Aboriginal people. There are times when eye contact is extremely inappropriate, for example, in certain kin relationships or between men and women who do not know each other. As a woman you may find it very refreshing to be able to walk past a large group of men without even a glance, let alone a whistle! It is very important not to embarrass people by staring. Remember that you may end up embarrassing yourself if your stares are interpreted as indicating sexual interest.

It is not polite to talk to a mother-to-be or a father-to-be about the child they are going to have. Aboriginal women may talk among themselves about pregnancy, but questions or interest from a stranger about this topic is likely to embarrass people into an awkward silence.

It is both offensive and upsetting for many Aboriginal people in central Australia to hear the name of a close relative or friend who has recently passed away. The deceased is often referred to by their 'skin' name, or by their relationship to other people. If someone has the same name, or a name that sounds the same as a person who has just passed away, then they may be given a new name, or they may be referred to as *kwementyaye* (Arrernte), *kumanjayi* (Warlpiri) or *kunmanara* (Pitjantjatjara). It is also offensive to show photographs of a person who has recently passed away.

Family Relationships

Aboriginal people in central Australia think of themselves as related to all the people in their own language group, and often to people in other language groups as well. To regulate social behaviour, law and ceremony, and relationship to land, Aboriginal societies are typically divided up into several sets of 'moieties' (essentially a moiety is a division of the society into two opposed and balanced halves). In many parts of northern Australia, the kinship and moiety groupings have been summarised in a neat and efficient way through what are commonly known as 'skin' groups or subsections. The most common pattern is for there to be eight 'skin' groups, often further divided into male and female groups (see the following chart). A person is born into one of these 'skin' groups and acquires the name of that 'skin' group as well as a personal name. Various relatives are classed together in each 'skin' group. A person's position within this system determines their relationship

Central Australian Aboriginal 'Skin' Names

LANGUAGE GROUPS	WESTERN DESERT NGAANYATJARRA	PINTUPI/ LURITJA	WARLPIRI	ARRERNTE & ANMATYERR
SECTION / SUB-SECTION — male	Yiparrka	Tjangala	Jangala	Angale
female		Nangala	Nangala	
SUB-SECTION — male	Panaka	Tjupurrula	Jupurrurla	Perrurle
female		Napurrula	Napurrurla	
Moiety 'Sun-side'				
SECTION / SUB-SECTION — male	Tjarurru	Tjungurrayi	Jungarrayi	Kngwarraye
female		Nungurrayi	Nungarrayi	
SUB-SECTION — male		Tjapanangka	Japanangka	Penangke
female		Napanangka	Napanangka	
SECTION / SUB-SECTION — male	Milangka	Tjampitjinpa	Jampijinpa	Ampetyane
female		Nampitjinpa	Nampijinpa	
SUB-SECTION — male	Karimarra	Tjakamarra	Jakamarra	Kemarre
female		Nakamarra	Nakamarra	
Moiety 'Shade-side'				
SECTION / SUB-SECTION — male	Purungu	Tjapangati	Japangardi	Pengarte
female		Napangati	Napangardi	
SUB-SECTION — male		Tjapaltjarri	Japaljarri	Peltharre
female		Napaltjarri	Napaljarri	

compiled by Robert Hoogenraad, Northern Territory Department of Education and social and ceremonial obligations to all others in the language group. Kinship systems are too complex to describe fully here. There are several books available that give an overview of kinship in central Australia, including *A Simple Introduction to Central Australian Kinship Systems* by Jim Wafer (IAD publications, 1982).

Travelling & Staying on Aboriginal Land

Apart from major town centres like Alice Springs and Tennant Creek, many Aboriginal people in central Australia live in remote communities and out-stations, many of which are on Aboriginal land. Most Aboriginal communities do not welcome visitors, except those people who have a genuine reason to visit (for example, people who are connected with Aboriginal organisations or government departments, or who have been invited by someone in the community).

Some communities have established tourism ventures, such as Wallace Rockhole, and Hermannsburg south-west of Alice Springs. For information about tour operators in the southern half of the Northern Territory, contact the Central Land Council (PO Box 3321, Alice Springs, 0871). For information about tour operators on the Anangu Pitjantjatjara Lands in the northern part of South Australia, contact: Anangu Pitjantjatjara (PMB Umuwa, via Alice Springs 0872); Desert Tracks (PO Box 360, Yulara, 0872); or the Aboriginal Tour Agency (PO Box 365, Alice Springs, 0871). You will need a permit to visit or travel through all communities on Aboriginal land in central Australia, and as this can sometimes take a few weeks to process, it is better to plan ahead.

If you are fortunate enough to have the opportunity to visit an Aboriginal community, don't leave the community on your own to go for a walk or do a bit of sightseeing. Ask an Aboriginal person to go with you. They will make sure that you do not stumble across any ceremonial camps or sacred areas that you should not see. Also, make an effort to dress appropriately — make sure that your clothes are clean, and avoid revealing or tight clothing.

Taking Photographs

It is important to observe the usual courtesies in taking photographs of people — make sure that you ask for permission first, and if practical, offer to send copies of the photographs to your subjects. It is also extremely important not to photograph sacred sites. In some popular tourist destinations, such as Uluru, there are signs at sacred sites requesting that you do not take photographs or use a video camera. Commercial photography and filming is prohibited in many areas. Contact the Central Land Council or Anangu Pitjantjatjara for details.

You are not allowed to carry alcohol into most central Australian Aboriginal communities. This rule is strictly enforced. If you are found carrying alcohol into a dry community your vehicle will be taken from you as penalty. Most vehicles are not returned, so it is very foolish to take this risk. Where this rule is in place, it applies to all people living in the community, both Aboriginal and non-Aboriginal.

Further Reading

There are several places in Alice Springs that stock a range of books about Aboriginal culture and languages, and some that also sell paintings and artefacts. A few of these are owned by Aboriginal groups. These include: IAD Press, (tel (089) 52 2688), 3 South Terrace, Alice Springs, and the CAAMA Shop, (tel (089) 55 5477), Alice Springs Airport; and (tel (089) 52 8773), Hartley St, Alice Springs (opposite the Post Office). All the books mentioned in this chapter are available from these outlets.

LANGUAGE GROUPS

The following are descriptions of three major language groups of the region

Arrernte

Languages & Dialects

The language name spelt Arrernte in the spelling system used to write in this language is perhaps better known outside central Australia as Aranda or Arunta. This language is part of a group of closely related languages and dialects known to linguists as the Arandic group. The major language in this group has a number of dialects, including Central, Eastern, Western and Southern Arrernte, Eastern and Western Anmatyerr and Eastern and Western Alyawarr. There are two smaller languages in the group, not so closely related: Kaytetye to the north and Lower Arrernte to the south. The territory of the group comprises very roughly the south eastern quarter of the Northern Territory (of which a fairly big chunk, the Simpson Desert, is uninhabitable), and also extends into South Australia north of Oodnadatta (see map below). Alice Springs is in Central Arrernte country. There are about 4500 speakers of languages of the group.

Sounds

The Arandic languages are believed to have had sound systems very much like their neighbouring languages, such as Warlpiri and Pitjantjatjara, at some time in the distant past, but they have changed drastically over the centuries. As an example, the word *wama* 'snake' has become *apmwe*, *apme* and *mwang* in various dialects.

Vowels

The most common vowel in Arandic languages is written **e**, but its pronunciation depends very much on what sounds come immedi-

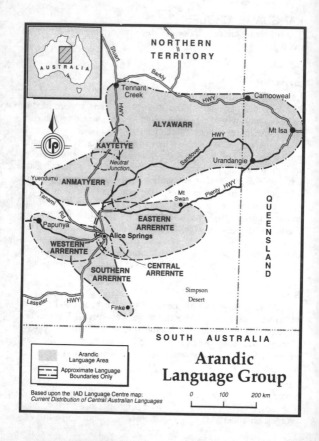

SOUTH AUSTRALIA

Arandic
Language Group

Arandic Language Area

Approximate Language Boundaries Only

Based upon the IAD Language Centre map:
Current Distribution of Central Australian Languages

0   100   200 km

ately before and after. Other vowels are **a** (similar to the **a** in 'father'), in some dialects; **i** (sounds like ' air' or like **ee** in 'see', depending on what the next consonant is); and **u** (pronounced like **u** in ' put' when it begins a word, or like **or** in 'more' when it comes after the first consonant).

Consonants

The consonant system is quite complicated, with a number of sounds that exist in almost no other Australian language. One unfortunate result, from the point of view of writing, is that some sounds which function as single sounds in these languages need to be written with two letters (such as **nh, ly, pm, tn, rr**) and some even need three letters (**kng, tnh, tny, rtn**).

Stress

Stress in Arandic languages is mostly on the vowel that follows the first consonant in a word, although in some dialects short words, such as *artwe* 'man' and *iltye* 'hand' are stressed on the initial vowel.

Structure

The languages of central Australia are basically similar in their grammar. The most obvious differences from English are the use of different endings on words where we would use prepositions (like 'to', 'for', 'with') in English, and the fact that the order of words in a sentence is nowhere near as fixed as in English. The endings tell us which words in a sentence are the subject and the object, and so changing the order of words does not change the meaning as it would in English. The endings differ from language to language but the systems are much the same. The basic grammar of Central Arrernte is described in the *A Learner's Guide to Eastern and Central Arrernte* by Jenny Green (IAD Press, 1994).

Arrernte Geography

The Arrernte name for the Alice Springs area is **Mparntwe**, while Heavitree Gap is **Ntaripe**. The MacDonnell Ranges as a whole are called **Tyurretye** (sometimes spelt Choritja). Prominent Central Australian mountains include: **Rwetyepme** (Mt Sonder), **Urlatherrke** (Mt Zeil) and **Alhekulyele** (Mt Gillen).

Other well-known scenic spots in Arrernte country include:

Eastern MacDonnell Ranges

Anthwerrke	Emily Gap
Kepalye	Jessie Gap
Inteyarrkwe	Ross River
Ilwentye	Ndhala Gorge

Western MacDonnell Ranges

Urrengetyirrpe	Simpsons Gap
Angkele	Standley Chasm
Twipethe	Ellery Creek Big Hole
Kwartetweme	Ormiston Gorge
Yaperlpe	Glen Helen Gorge

Arrernte placenames are of two types. One type is when the name describes the place; for example, the Finke River is **Lherepirnte** (anglicised as Larapinta). This is composed of *lhere* 'river' and *pirnte* 'salt' (although there is some doubt about this, as *pirnte* means 'spring (of water)' in some dialects). Likewise, Finke is **Aperturl**, (usually spelled Aputula), which translates as 'hill-forehead' and refers to a nearby hill.

The second type of name is taken from the Dreaming (or Aboriginal creation history) of the area. For example, an area in Alice Springs is called **Ntyarlkarletyaneme** 'the place where the elephant grub crosses over'. **Ntyarlke**, the elephant grub, is one of the ancestral caterpillar beings which created much of the landscape around Alice Springs (as well as being a caterpillar that still occurs in the area). Some hills in the area covered by the name are parts of the body of these ancestral beings (see the signs at the golf course). Further east, in the MacDonnell Ranges, **Anthwerrke**, the name for Emily Gap means 'small intestine' and refers to the guts of the caterpillar.

Vocabulary

Some words that you may come across during your visit are:

arelhe or *tyerrtye*	Aboriginal person
lhentere or *warlpele*	non-Aboriginal person
altyerre	Dreaming, the Law
inernte	beads
urtne	coolamon (a shallow wooden dish)
irrtyarte	spear
alye	boomerang
atneme	women's digging stick
kwatye	water
merne	food, especially vegetable foods and bread
utyerrke	bush fig
akatyerre	desert raisin
pmerlpe	quandong (edible fruit)
untyeye	corkwood
kere	meat or animal used for food
aherre	red plains kangaroo
atyunpe	perentie (large lizard)

rapite	rabbit
arlewatyerre	sand goanna
tyape	edible grubs
ntyarlke	elephant grub
yeperenye	caterpillar that lives on the tar vine
ngkwarle	sweet things
yerrampe	honey ant

References

The following books are all available through IAD Press and local bookshops — see page 104 for details.

Green, J 1993 *Alyawarr to English Dictionary,* IAD Press.

Green, J 1994 *A Learner's Guide to Eastern and Central Arrernte,* IAD Press.

Henderson, J 1991 *A Learner's Wordlist of Eastern and Central Arrernte,* IAD Press.

Henderson, J & Dobson, V 1994 *Eastern and Central Arrernte to English Dictionary,* IAD Press.

Swan, C & Cousens, M 1993 *A Learner's Wordlist of Pertame,* IAD Press

The Arrernte Landscape of Alice Springs by David Brooks (IAD Press, 1991) gives readers an insight into the traditional history of Mparntwe (Alice Springs), and offers a fascinating travelogue of the Alice Springs region. To follow the text of the booklet, readers need to climb Anzac Hill and Annie Meyer Hill to get a view over the town area. *Arrernte Foods: foods from Central Australia* by Margaret-Mary Turner (IAD Press, 1994), an Arrernte woman fluent in Eastern and Central Arrernte, takes a comprehensive look at traditional bush foods from Mparntwe and surrounding areas. IAD Press plans to publish a phrasebook of central Australian languages in 1995. This phrasebook will assist visitors to central Australia in pronouncing commonly used words and phrases from local languages, including Arrernte, Western Desert languages and Warlpiri.

Western Desert Language
Languages & Dialects
The Western Desert Language spreads over a vast area of desert country (see map, page 112). Dialects of Western Desert include Pitjantjatjara, Yankunytjatjara, Ngaanyatjarra, Ngaatjatjarra, Pintupi, Papunya Luritja, Luritja, Matutjara, Kukatja, Antikirinya, Mantjiltjara and Kartutjara.

In all, it is estimated that there are between 4000 and 5000 speakers of Western Desert dialects, with Pitjantjatjara being one of the better known varieties. Most of the Pitjantjatjara and Yankunytjatjara people live on the Anangu Pitjantjatjara freehold lands in the north-west of South Australia, or just over the borders in Western Australia and the Northern Territory.

Visitors to central Australia are likely to meet speakers of Pitjantjatjara and Yankunytjatjara at Uluru (Ayers Rock) and Kata Tjuta (the Olgas), and Pitjantjatjara and Luritja speakers at Watarrka (Kings Canyon).

Sounds
The examples of sounds given here are all from Pitjantjatjara or Yankunytjatjara. All other Western Desert dialects also contain these sounds, although there are some minor variations in spelling and pronunciation.

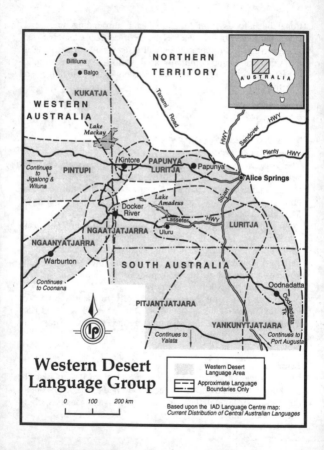

Western Desert Language Group

Vowel

Dialects of Western Desert contain three vowel sounds: **a**, **i** and **u**. These are like the sounds in 'father', 'hid' and 'put' in standard Australian English. Each sound may vary slightly according to the surrounding consonants. Long varieties of each vowel sound are written as **aa**, **ii** and **uu**.

Consonants

As with all central Australian languages, there are sounds in Western Desert language that are not found in English. Probably one of the hardest sounds for the English speaker to produce is the **ng** sound when it occurs at the beginning of a word such as *ngura* (home or camp). The **g** is not a hard sound as in 'finger' — it is more like the **ng** in the middle of 'singer'. The underlined letters indicate retroflex or 'r-coloured' sounds (see page 91 of the Introduction). There are several other consonant sounds that you may find tricky. Language learners usually find it easier to learn to pronounce words correctly by listening carefully to a speaker of the language, rather than learning from a book.

Stress

Stress in Western Desert dialects usually falls on the first syllable of a word. In long words, other syllables may also be stressed, but never as much as the first syllable.

Structure

Most dialects of Western Desert have a similar or related structure, but use different vocabulary, and some different forms of grammatical endings. The most obvious difference between the structure of these dialects and English is in word order and the use of case markers. Where word order is significant in English to mark subject and object, Western Desert dialects use case markers to mark subject and object. This means that word order is much freer than it is in English. Other elements of structure are too complex to describe here, but there are several reference books available through IAD to assist language learners.

Uluṟu & Kaṯa Tjuṯa

Both of these landmarks are on the border between Pitjantjatjara and Yankunytjatjara country. The name **Uluṟu** is thought by some people to be derived from *ulerenye*, an Arrernte word for 'stranger'. **Kaṯa Tjuṯa** translates into English as 'heads' or 'many heads'. There are signs around the base of Uluṟu and at Kaṯa Tjuṯa in Pitjantjatjara, with English translations. An excellent way to learn more about the language and culture is to take the Liru Walk or one of the other guided walks run by the Australian Nature Conservation Agency.

Pitjantjatjara and Yankunytjatjara people call tourists *minga tjuta* (ants). If you stand at the base of Uluṟu, and watch people climbing you will understand why. Although it is not widely advertised, the traditional owners of Uluṟu would prefer that you didn't climb the rock. There is a sign explaining this at the base of the climb. Apart from the damage being caused to sacred sites, the traditional owners are worried about the number of people that have been killed or injured during the climb.

Vocabulary

Some words that you may come across during your visit are:

anangu	Aboriginal person
piṟanpa or *walypala*	non-Aboriginal person
tjukurpa	Dreaming, the Law
ininti	beads
piti	coolamon (wooden bowl used to carry water)

katji or *kulata*	spear
kali	boomerang
wana	women's digging stick
kapi	water
mai	food, especially vegetable foods and bread
ili	bush fig
kampurarpa	desert raisin
wayanu	quandong
witjinti	corkwood
kuka	meat or animal used for food
malu	red plains kangaroo
ngintaka	perentie
rapita	rabbit
tinka	sand goanna
maku	edible grubs
anumara	edible caterpillar
maku	witchetty grub (grub that lives in the roots of the witchetty bush)
wama	sweet things, nowadays also used to refer to alcohol
tjala	honey ant
kurku	honeydew on mulga (an acacia shrub)

Watarrka

Watarrka (Kings Canyon) is in Luritja country, and takes its name from a type of acacia known as the umbrella bush (*Acacia ligulata*) that grows in the valley below the canyon. There are signs around the canyon walk in Pitjantjatjara, with English translations. You can learn more about the language and culture of people from this area by taking one of the tours organised by Kurkara Tours based at the resort (Kings Canyon Frontier Lodge).

References

The following books are all available through IAD Press and local bookshops — see page 104 for details.

Eckert, P & Hudson, J *Wangka Wiṟu: A handbook for the Pitjantjatjara language learner*, University of South Australia

Goddard, C 1992 *Pitjantjatjara/Yankunytjatjara to English Dictionary,* IAD Publications

Hansen, K.C. & L.E. 1992 *Pintupi/Luritja Dictionary,* IAD Publications

Amee Glass has written a booklet called *Into Another World: A glimpse of the Culture of the Ngaanyatjarra People of Central Australia* (IAD Press, 1993) about living with Ngaanyatjarra people from Warburton, which is just over 200 kilometres west of the Northern Territory border in Western Australia. This booklet contains some very useful information, much of which is also relevant to relating to people from other language groups, particularly other Western Desert languages.

WARLPIRI
Languages & Dialects

There are thought to be at least 3000 Warlpiri, most of whom speak Warlpiri as their first language. They live in a number of quite large communities around the edge of traditional Warlpiri country: **Yurntumu** (Yuendumu), **Lajamanu** (which used to be called Hooker Creek, and is actually on Kurindji country), **Wirliyajar**.

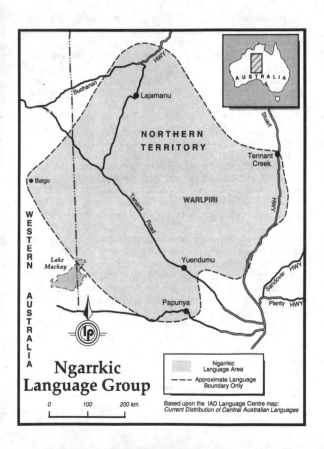

Ngarrkic Language Group

0   100   200 km

Ngarrkic Language Area

Approximate Language Boundary Only

Based upon the IAD Language Centre map: Current Distribution of Central Australian Languages

rayi (Willowra) and **Nyirrpi** (which is strictly speaking a Pintupi community). But many Warlpiri spend at least part of the year in the many small out-stations in Warlpiri country, the heart of which is the Tanami Desert, named by Europeans after **Janami** rock-hole, near the junction of the Tanami road and the Lajamanu road. There are also very substantial Warlpiri populations in other communities around traditional Warlpiri country, especially **Alekarenge** on Kaytetye country (a Kaytetye name referring to 'Dog Dreaming', also written Ali Curung and which used to be called Warrabri), and in towns such as Alice Springs on Arrernte country, Tennant Creek on Warumungu country, and Katherine on Jawoyn country.

Warlpiri is still a very vigorous language, and though it is being lost by Warlpiri children in some communities that lie outside the traditional country, usually for Aboriginal English or an Aboriginal creole, it is none the less spreading well outside its traditional country, and is also spoken by 1000 or more people as a second language over a very large area, extending as far north as Darwin, west to Fitzroy crossing in WA, east to Tennant creek and other Barkly Tableland communities, and south to Alice Springs and the northern Western Desert communities.

There are five major dialects of Warlpiri: Warrmarla or Ngardilypa was spoken to the west, Warnayaka to the north, Ngaliya to the south, Yarlpiri or Warlpiri in the Lander River area in the heart of Warlpiri country, and Wakirti Warlpiri in the Hansen River area to the east. The main differences are in vocabulary and pronunciation, reflecting the influences of neighbouring languages, but they are mutually comprehensible. Though the Warlpiri will sometimes emphasise the dialect differences, they generally consider themselves to be one people with one language, Warlpiri.

Sounds

Warlpiri has a spelling system which has been in use since 1974, mainly in the context of bilingual education programs in the schools of the main Warlpiri communities. Nowadays, most young and even middle-aged Warlpiri can read and write their language.

Vowels

Warlpiri has only three vowels, written **i**, **u** and **a**. The **u** sound has the European pronunciation, like **oo** in 'zoo'. Long varieties of each vowel sound are written as **ii**, **uu** and **aa**.

Consonants

The 'retroflex' sounds **rt**, **rn**, and **rl** are pronounced with the tongue-tip curled right back, so that the bottom of the tongue tip touches the roof of the mouth. Warlpiri has three 'r's: **r**, **rr** and **rd**. The **rr** represents a trilled 'r'; **rd** is a retroflex 'r', made with the tongue flicked forward rapidly. The sound **ng** represents the sound in 'si**ng**er', never that in 'fi**ng**er'.

Stress

Stress always falls on the first syllable of the word. Words in Warlpiri are always at least two syllables long, and must end in a vowel, so words borrowed from English can be quite hard to recognise: eg *kuurlu* (school) and *wijipirtili* (hospital).

Structure

Warlpiri has a complex grammar: for instance it has a case system (a set of categories for nouns, etc), five verb classes and a complex tense system. Although its system of counting is poorly developed, it makes extensive use of a distinction between singular (one), dual (two, a pair) and plural (more than two) in both the grammar and kinship system. There are several reference books available from IAD to assist language learners.

Vocabulary

Some words that you may come across during your visit are:

yapa	Aboriginal person
kardiya	non-Aboriginal person
jukurrpa	Dreaming, the Law
karli	boomerang
parraja	coolamon, used to winnow (separate grains and chaff), carry food, and as a baby carrier
ngapa	water
mangarriyi or *miyi*	food, especially vegetable foods and bread
ngurlu	seeds, grain
ngayaki	bush tomato
yarla	bush potato
kuyu	meat or animal used for food
marlu	red plains kangaroo
yankirri	emu
wardapi	sand goanna
pama	delicacy, nowadays also used to refer to alcohol
jurlarda	bush honey
ngarlkirdi	witchetty grub

References

IAD Press publishes Warlpiri learning materials, including the *Learner's Guide to Warlpiri* (in preparation at the time of publication). A very large encyclopaedic Warlpiri dictionary has been in preparation over the last 15 years and is expected to be published in 1995. Warlpiri is probably the best researched Australian Aboriginal language: a bibliography of published and unpublished works is available from IAD.

Northern Australian Languages

Introduction

The 'Top End' is a colourful term which can be used to refer to the northern half of the Northern Territory, since it's at the 'top' of a map of Australia. Although it is a useful term to refer to this area on a map, it might suggest that the 'Top End' is somehow geographically and culturally homogeneous, but this is definitely not the case.

The region encompasses a great variety of different environments – saltwater coastal areas, subcoastal flood plains, inland rock plateau and escarpment country, freshwater river systems, open savannah and grasslands, dry inland deserts. Each environment is populated with its own distinct plants and animals. Just as the climate has influenced the type and diversity of plant and animal life in the region, it has influenced in profound ways the life of its Aboriginal inhabitants: population density, the degree to which people were nomadic, hunting and gathering techniques and associated material culture, trade routes (and therefore the routes of diffusion for innovations in culture and language) and so on. Just as the country in the Top End displays great ecological diversity, so its Aboriginal inhabitants have many distinct cultural and linguistic traditions.

The Top End is the home of a great many Aboriginal languages. Some are related to other languages traditionally spoken on the Australian mainland, like the Yolŋu languages of the north-east, which are related too ther Pama-Nyungan languages. (For an explanation of the Pama-Nyungan and non-Pama-Nyungan languages, see the Introduction, page 90.) Others belong to language families confined to the Top End, that is, the various Top End language families collectively referred to as non-Pama-Nyungan).

Yet other Top End languages appear to be language 'isolates' – unrelated to any other language of the region – for instance, Tiwi.

Members of a Language Group may speak a distinct language or they may speak a dialect (and can consequently understand the speech of other Language Group/s). Membership in a particular Language Group carries important social and ceremonial significance. It is inherited through either or both parents (depending on the area), implies the right to or ownership of a particular language or dialect and it (along with other social factors) grants responsibility for and ownership of certain areas, ceremonies and songs.

Travellers in the Top End are often intrigued by the numbers of Language Groups represented in this region, but really this is a matter of 'relativity'. Linguistic situations comparable or even more diverse to that in the Top End can be seen in the tropics to the north of Australia. The island containing Irian Jaya and Papua New Guinea, for example, contains 20% of the world's languages.

Historical Influences
Macassans

During the last two centuries before European invasion, Aboriginal peoples of the north coast of Australia had regular interaction with people from further north. These people, known as 'Macassans', came south every year for trepang – 'bêches de mer'. The legacy of their visits is found in material items, family ties, language and ceremony. Their voyages ceased in 1906 when they were banned by the Australian government. In recent times, contact has been re-established through activities such as people from Yolŋu communities visiting Veljang Pandang ('Macassar') where they met relatives. In 1988, a prau (canoe-like sailing boat) re-enacted the voyages of old, bringing relatives and others from 'Macassar' to old hunting grounds and families in East Arnhem Land.

Words from Makassarese are found in many northern languages. Examples from the Yolŋu languages include:

rrupiya   money (Macassar: *rupiya*, money)
bathala   big, important (Macassar: *bàttala*, heavy, big, onorous)
detuh   (pronounced diitung) buffalo
               (Macassar: *tèdong*, carabar, water buffalo)

European Invasion

The history of the European invasion of the Top End is important to the understanding of the present linguistic situation. In areas where Europeans settled early and in large numbers, such as around the Darwin region and along a corridor extending southwards following the Stuart Highway, local languages are no longer spoken.

In the drier open savannah country, cattle stations were set up using the labour of Aboriginal people. It is difficult to generalise on the effect that cattle stations had on Top End Language Groups. Aboriginal station 'employees' (wage and living conditions often amounted to little better than slave labour) had to be able to communicate in English. Where Aboriginal station 'employees' were predominately from the same Language Group (eg. Wave Hill Station and the Gurindji Language Group or Elsey Station and the Mangarrayi Language Group) it was possible for people to continue speaking their traditional language in some situations, such as in the camp or when out bush. The seasonal nature of station work – there was little or no work available during the Wet – also meant that Aboriginal 'employees' used their traditional knowledge to survive.

Around the Top End coastline, missions were established; their effec on the Aboriginal Language Groups depended much on the individual institution. In some instances, missionaries forbade the use of traditional languages, in others, Europeans working with a mission were expected to learn the traditional languages. At some missions, the so-called 'dormitory system' was enforced whereby children were housed separately from their parents in dormitories. This was particularly disruptive to the transmission of traditional languages, especially where children were from many different Language Groups.

Present-Day Situation

Top End languages provide examples of all possible post-colonial fates of indigenous languages – from no speakers at all to full use in all everyday activities.

In areas with large, long-term European settlement (eg. Darwin or Katherine) the traditional languages are no longer spoken. Traditional Aboriginal languages are still spoken in geographically isolated areas, where contact with non-Aboriginal people has been most recent and where there are relatively few non-Aboriginal settlers. These Areas include the Daly River Region south-west of Darwin, the Arnhem Land Reserve to the east and the desert region at the south-western periphery of the Top End. In areas with a lot of non-Aboriginal visitors such as Kakadu National Park, only older members of the Aboriginal Community know their ancestral languagesfluently; younger people tend to understand and use some traditional language, but speak mostly Kriol, a dialect of Aboriginal English or another traditional language.

Language Shift

Establishment of large permanent communities this century through missions, reserves or cattle stations has seen shifts in the traditional use and acquisition of languages. In some remote areas, linguistic diversity is maintained. However, in most of the larger communities one language has become the language of common use. This may be a local language, Kriol or a koine – a new local language resulting from contact of traditional languages. This shift has not necessarily been to the exclusion of all (other) traditional languages and there is widespread concern about the maintenance of these.

In communities where traditional languages continue to be used, some traditional languages are growing in numbers of speakers while others are declining. This is due to language shifts from one traditional language to another, in part because of changing demographic patterns. Formerly, small numbers of people lived in isolated clan groups and this isolation fostered the maintenance of many distinct language varieties. These days, even in isolated areas, people tend to live for at least some of the year at large regional communities populated by members of many different language groups. In these multilingual communities people experience a need for a common language and one traditional language gradually emerges as the 'lingua franca' of the community. At Maningrida community in central-coastal Arnhem Land where there are members of at least eight different language groups, two of the local languages are gradually emerging as lingua francas: one used by people who affiliate with the 'west side' (Kunwinjku and its eastern dialects) and the other used by people who affiliate with the 'east side' (Burarra). Children growing up at Maningrida community tend to learn one of these emergent lingua francas because these are the languages which enable them to communicate with the largest number of people.

The influence of European institutions such as the Church and schools has also affected this type of language shift in some com-munities.' At Wadeye in the Daly River region members of eight traditional language groups moved in from traditional country to live at the mission. Missionaries encouraged the use of Murrinh-patha, language of the traditional owners of the country in which the mission was located. A Murrinh-patha bible was produced; linguists and language workers produced a dictionary and other documentary materials and the school introduced a bilingual education program in Murrinh-patha. Between the '60s to '90s, Murrinh-patha gradually became the standard language of the whole community. An unintended side effect of this process of standardisation has now become apparent: very few young people speak any community language other than Murrinh-patha fluently, and almost no children understand community languages other than Murrinh-patha. The school and the regional language centre have recently begun work on documentation of the other community languages.

Kriol

Another form of language shift that has occurred in the Top End is the widespread use of Kriol throughout most of the Katherine Region and westwards as far as Broome. Kriol arose out of the social situation created at the Roper River Mission to which many Aboriginal peoples from south-eastern Arnhem Land were relocated. An additional factor to the mixing of a great variety of language groups in accelerating the whole process of language change, was the dormitory system in operation there.

Kriol, for the most part is a spoken language, although it has been used as a language of instruction in the bilingual school program at Barunga Community, where many texts have been produced. There is also a Kriol Bible translation and a Kriol-English dictionary available. The Barunga band, Blekbala Mujik, and other bands from communities in Katherine region have used Kriol in their songs. Kriol is still often stigmatised, however, as a non-standard or sub-standard variety of English, whereas it is actually a new and full language in its own right.

Kriol has elements in common with traditional Aboriginal languages, with English and with other creole languages. Creole languages, as new languages, tend to have fewer of the 'irregularities' that occur in older languages. The influence of traditional languages on Kriol is observable in the sound system, many vocabulary items (especially for domains of traditional knowledge like relationship terms, native plants and animals, and everyday words for things like parts of the body) and structural features. The vocabulary items typically drawn from traditional languages tend to reflect the language background of the speakers and communities. The use of *mayin*, 'food, tucker', for example, would indicate the Kriol speaker came from the western areas.

Kriol has also drawn a large amount of vocabulary from English, but non-Kriol speakers should be aware that words seemingly of English origin do not necessarily have the same meaning in Kriol. For instance, the Kriol word *kilim* means 'hit, beat' and *not* 'kill'.

Land Rights

In recent years, many Aboriginal Language Groups have been able to claim (part of) their traditional lands through the Aboriginal Land Rights (N.T.) Act of 1976. Due to the provisions of this legislation, about the kind of land able to be claimed and about who may be recognised as traditional owners, not all Aboriginal groups have been able to regain possession of their land. (The effect in the Top End of the 1992 supreme court decision on Mabo, which has finally recognised indigenous peoples' land tenure, is as yet unknown.)

It was in part the regaining of the ownership of and access to traditional lands which made the 'Homeland Centres' movement possible.(Homeland Centres is the term commonly used in the north-east region. In other areas, the term 'outstation' is in use – in some instances for the same kind of smaller community, in some instances for a less permanent 'base' in a group's traditional country.) This movement began in the '70s, saw family groups opting to move out of larger communities to their tradititional lands to start 'Homeland Centres' with populations of 15 to a hundred.

It should be noted that access to Aboriginal land and communities is restricted and monitored by a system of permits. Intending visitors must apply in advance to the relevant land council or community council – the Northern Land Council for most of the Top End, Anindilyakwa Land Council on Groote Eylandt or Central Land Council for some of the more southerly areas.

THE LANGUAGES
Katherine Region

In the Katherine Region, Aboriginal people nowadays use the terms 'sun-go-down' (or 'sunset') to refer to the peoples, lands and languages in the western Katherine region (approximately west of the Stuart Highway) and 'sun-rise' to refer to those to the east. This division reflects the perceived differences in languages, which way the various language groups 'look' (i.e. who they are affiliated with), traditional culture, the differences in climate and country and even in art styles (abstract 'dot paintings' are typical of the western Katherine region, whereas figures and lined artwork typify the east side).

The township of Katherine is the administrative centre of the region, and there are members of possibly all the language groups of the Katherine Region, and further afield, living in the township. Of the two traditional languages spoken in and around Katherine, Dagoman is no longer spoken and Jawoyn is spoken only by some older people. Traditional languages, such as Warlpiri or Rembarrnga, from the Katherine Region (and elsewhere) may be heard in the town.

The most common 'Aboriginal' language which a visitor to Katherine will hear will be Kriol. With the exception of remote communities, such as Lajamanu and Bulmun, the Aboriginal communities of the Katherine Region have Kriol as a first or main language.

Sun-go-down

The country is drier here than elsewhere in the Top End and the Victoria River is the one major river system. Due to the nature of the country, many large cattle stations have operated in the region. There are four major groupings of the Aboriginal population on the sun-go-down side of the Katherine Region: (south to north) Lajamanu, Daguragu/Kalkaringi, Yarralin and Timber Creek.

Lajamanu is nowadays a Warlpiri-speaking community because White authorities moved large numbers of Warlpiri people away from their traditional homeland farther south onto lands traditionally owned by Kartangarrurru and Gurindji people. (See the Central Australianchapter for information on Warlpiri.) Kartangarrurru is no longer spoken, but Gurindji is still spoken at Daguragu Community (the old strike camp) and at Kalkaringi (the old government settlement of Wave Hill). The Gurindji people are famous for the Wave Hill Strike of 1966 which fought back at the shocking wage and living conditions endured by Aboriginal people working on Top End cattle stations, andeventuated into a fight for land rights.

Situated to the east of Gurindji is the related language Mudbura which is spoken across as far as Elliot. To the north are the languages Bilinara (spoken mainly at Pigeon Hole Community) and Ngarinyman (spoken at Yarralin and outstations, north to Timber Creek and west as far as Kununurra). Gurindji, Bilianra and Ngarinyman are closely-related languages.

The traditional countries of four Language Groups converges around the Timber Creek area: Ngarinyman, Ngaliwurru, Nungali and Jaminjung. Traditional country for the Ngaliwurru Language Group also includes the spectacular Stokes Ranges. Nungali appears to be a severely threatened language with very few speakers remaining. Jaminjung, a non-Pama-Nyungan Language, is spoken up into the Daly Region.

To the east of Victoria River lies the traditional country of the Wardaman Language Group, although nowadays most Wardaman people live in and around the town of Katherine. Wardaman was mutually intelligible with the traditional languages near Katherine and Mataranka, Dagoman and Yangman respectively. Whereas Dagoman and Yangman are no longer spoken due to their location at points of early and extensive European settlement, Wardaman is still spoken and/or understood by younger people.

Sun-rise

The 'sun-rise' side of the Katherine region (south to north) goes from 'dry country' north of the Barkly Tableland, to 'freshwater country' associated with the Roper and Katherine River systems and their tributaries to the 'stone country' of the southern and eastern fringes of the Arnhem escarpment. Major Aboriginal Communities with their own elected councils are (south to north) Borroloola, Minyerri, Jilkminggan, Ngukurr, Barunga and Beswick. The 'sun-rise' languages of the Katherine region are all non-Pama-Nyungan languages.

The traditional language of Borroloola is Yanyuwa. An interesting feature of Yanyuwa is that women's speech is structurally different to the variety spoken by men. For instance, if a woman is talking about a male, then she must use the prefix ny(a)- on the noun and any adjectives referring to him. The structure of women's speech is considered by Yanyuwa speakers more complex than men's.

woman speaking	man speaking
*yenta **ny**artu **nya**morto*	*yenta artu morto*
you boy deaf (= disobedient)	you boy deaf (= disobedient)
'You disobedient boy!'	'You disobedient boy!'

To the north of Borroloola is the community of Ngukurr and several smaller surrounding communities. The linguistic situation here is highly complex. Numerous Language Groups now reside in these communities, including Ngalakan (the traditional landowners of Ngukurr), Alawa, Marra, Warndarrang, Nunggubuyu, Ritharrngu, Ngandi, Rembarrnga. Of these languages, Warndarrang is no longer spoken, Ngandi and Ngalakan have very few speakers, and Alawa and Marra are spoken by some people over about 50 years of age. Rembarrnga and Ritharrngu have speakers in more remote communities.

The communities of Minyerri (Hodgson Downs) and Jilkminggan are traditionally associated with the Alawa and Mangarrayi Language Groups repectively. Mangarrayi, like the Alawa and Marra languages, is nowadays spokenfluently only by some people over about the age of 50.

The communities of Barunga and Beswick were formerly part of Bamyili, a government reserve. The traditional Language group of this area is Jawoyn. Other Language Groups including Dalabon and Rembarrnga form a large proportion of the population. Jawoyn and Dalabon are no longer spoken by many people and are endangered. Rembarrnga, however, has many speakers in communities in Arnhem Land.

Central Region

Most of the Languages spoken in the interior part of the top end are related to one another as members of the Kunwinjkuan family. Languages in this family include Warray, Jawoyn, Mayali/Kunwinjku (and it's Eastern dialects Kuninjku, Kune), Kunbarlang, Rembarrnga, Dalabon (also called Dangbon and Ngalkbon), Ngalakan, Ngandi and Ngunggubuyu.

Kunwinjkuan Languages are spoken around the Arnhem Land Escarpment.

Warray is spoken by a few elderly people in the Pine Creek area. Jawoyn is spoken by some older people in Katherine, Pine Creek, Barunga and Beswick, around the south-western edge of the escarpment. The Jawoyn Language group has become well known as the traditional owners of the popular tourist destinations of Nitmiluk (Katherine Gorge) and Leliny (Edith Falls).

Mayali is a series of dialects spoken around the western and northern rim of the escarpment; these are called Mayali in the west, Kunwinjku in the north-west (Gunbalnya area), Kuninjku in the Liverpool River area and Kune on the northern half of the escarpment.

Dalabon is a central escarpment language whose country adjoins Rembarrnga, along the eastern edge of the escarpment. Dalabon and Rembarrnga are today spoken on the northern rim of the escarpment at Homeland centres such as Korlobidahda, Buluh Karduru, Manjangarnak and also at Communities situated south of the escarpment, such as Bulman, Beswick and Barunga.

Both the Ngalakan and Ngandi languages, once spoken around the south-east, along the Roper River, are severely endangered, with only a few elderly speakers.

Kunwinjkuan languages are famous because of the way that their words are constructed. In Kunwinjkuan languages words carry a lot of 'add-on' bits called 'affixes' that add extra components of meaning to simple word roots. Some affixes go on the front of the word and are called 'prefixes'. Other affixes go on the end of the word and are called 'suffixes'.

In Kunwinjkuan languages the prefixes are especially complex and interesting.Most Kunwinjkuan languages have a system of 'grammatical gender' which linguists call 'noun class systems'. French has two classes, 'masculine' and 'feminine'; German has a third – 'neuter'. Most of the Kunwinjkuan noun class languages have four classes; 'masculine, feminine, plant and inanimate'. The noun class is coded with a prefix on nouns and adjectives.

Noun class agreement in Kunbarlang:

kirdimarrk **na**-*rleng*	lots of men ('masculine')
barramimbanj **ki**-*rleng*	lots of women ('feminine')
mardugudj **ma**-*rieng*	lots of plums ('plant')
kuwalak **ku**-*rleng*	lots of rocks ('inanimate')

Northern Kunwinjkuan languages (Mayali, Kunwinjku, Kunbarlang) have 'free word order' in the sentence and no 'noun cases'; all the work of tracking 'who is doing what to whom' is done using the prefixes on the verb.

Southern Kunwinjkuan languages (Warray, Jawoyn, Dalabon, Rembarrnga, Ngalakan, Ngandi, Nunggu-buyu) have 'case endings' on nouns as well as 'prefixes on verbs'. Most of these languages however do not have noun classes.

Daly Region

Languages of the Daly region, south-west of Darwin, belong to several groups. Research is currently underway to establish the 'family' relationships between them. These languages have several unique grammatical features that are not found elsewhere in Aboriginal languages.

Firstly, they have 'fricative' (hissing) sounds. Fricative sounds are made by bringing two parts of the mouth together so that they are very 'close' but not quite 'touching'; this causes 'turbulent airflow' and a 'hissing' noise. (English 'fricatives' are spelt with the letters 'f, v, s, z, th and h'.) Of course fricative sounds in languages of the Daly region are a little different from the ones we use in English.

Secondly, Daly languages have nominal classifiers (Thai is another very famous classifier language). Classifiers are words with a very general meaning, such as 'person', 'animal', 'tree', 'liquid', 'thing'. The grammar requires that every ordinary noun, such as the name of an animal or a variety of tree, occur together with a classifier. The examples used here all from the Mati Ke language of the Wadeye area.

me	higher animates; sentient beings (live people and spirits)
awu	animals, also any people to whom you wish to refer in a derogatory way
miyi	vegetable foods
thawurr	trees; wooden things; long rigid cylindrical objects.
nhanjdji	things (objects); natural substances (rock, sand, wind, sun)
yeri	implements of war and destruction (lightning, weapons); *yeri tjendi*, spears and blades
wudi	liquids (bodies of water, drinks, tea, beer)
wuyi	locations (times and places)
marri	speech and language

Cross-Classification

Some noun stems can be used with more than one classifier. Changing the classifier changes the reference of the noun. In many cases it is possible to see that the meanings of the two different combinations of classifier-plus-noun are related:

awu kulemin	long – bum, 'animal' class. This is a mollusc, which is eaten.
nhandji kulemin	long – bum shell, 'thing' class
nhandji babar lthang	red-flowering kurrajong tree, also the inner bark used to make string, 'thing' class
miyi babarlthang	edible seeds of the red-flowering kurrajong, 'vegetable food' class

In other cases the same noun stem is used with different classifiers and the two noun-plus-classifier combinations seem to have quite distinct meanings. To a foreigner there may seem to be no connection between the two meanings; how ever there may be culture-specific conventions which link the two:

nhandji marri	cycad plant ('thing' class)
miyi marri	ripe cycad nuts ('food' class)
awu marri	bush cockroach; lives in dead cycads fronds ('animal' class)
me marri	a cycad/cockroach person (a person who belongs to the cycad/cockroach totem. The cycad and the cockroach belong together in atotemic complex. You can't have one as a totem without also having the other.)

Darwin & the North Coast

Larrakiya is the language of the traditional owners of Darwin. Today it is spoken by only a few elderly people. For other languages of the Darwin region, the situation is the same. You will certainly hear many different Aboriginal languages spoken on the streets of Darwin, but none of them will be Larrakiya. The languages you will hear will be indigenous to other areas, spoken by people who are immigrants or visitors to the town. Members of the Larrakiya community are currently working to record and revive their ancestral language. Larrakiya words are used in songs written and performed by the Darwin group, The Mills Sisters.

Tiwi continues to be spoken on Bathurst and Melville Islands immediately to the north of Darwin. Bathurst Island is a popular tourist destination and texts produced in Tiwi language are available for purchase by visitors.

Along the coast to the east of Darwin are several different groups of languages. We know very little of any of the languages spoken west of Kakadu. Only very old people still speak the languages of Kakadu and the Gurig Peninsula; most younger people now speak Mayali/Kunwinjku. On the islands off the coast of western Arnhem Land, Iwadja and Maung are spoken. Kunbarlang is a coastal relative of Kunwinjku and was spoken west of the Liverpool River, however, most young Barlang people now speak Kunwinjku. There is a small language group comprising distant relatives of the Kunwinjkuan family spoken in the area around Maningrida in central coastal Arnhem Land, between the Liverpool and the Blyth Rivers. These are Ndjebbana (also called Kunibidji), Nakkara, Burarra, Gun-narpta and Gurrgoni.

Maningrida Community is an important regional centre and is situated in a transitional area between east and west Arnhem Land.

There are significant cultural differences between Arnhem Landers who affiliate with the 'west side' and those who affiliate with the 'east side'. Burarra people affiliate with the 'east side' and the Burarra language has been used in popular music recently recorded by the Maningrida Sunrize Band.

North-East Arnhem

Much of the north-east of the Territory is part of Arnhem Land, a reserve established in 1933 and granted Aboriginal title under the Aboriginal Land Rights Act (N.T.) of 1976. The Aboriginal population is distributed between eight main communities (Ramingining, Milingimbi, Gapuwiyak, Galiwin'ku, Yirrkala, Umbakumba, Angurugu and Numbulwar) and numerous homeland centres. Most non-Aborigines in the region are there for work, either in Aboriginal communities (eg. schools, clinics etc) or in the two mining towns (Nhulunbuy or Alyangula). Since the '70s, when self-determination came on to the political agenda, an increasing number of Aboriginal people are holding positions previously held by non-Aborigines.

The languages of the north-east corner of Arnhem Land are of the Pama-Nyungan type. They have become commonly known outside the region as the Yolŋu (yuulŋu) languages. In this area, each clan claims to have a distinct language variety and there are some 50 clans. The relationship of these languages to each other is complex. A useful starting point is to think of a patchwork quilt in which some materials appear at different places on the quilt. Instead of materials imagine a network of lands belonging to different clans woven together by spiritual, ceremonial and linguistic threads made by the Ancestral Beings. Land, clan, song, ceremony and languages are all linked together.

There is a local way of grouping different clan language varieties which parallels linguistic ideas of language groupings. This groups together different clan languages according to the word they use for 'this' or 'here' eg. clans such as Gälpu (Gaalpu), Rirratjiŋu (Rirratjingu), Golomala (Guulumala) and Wangurri (Wangurri) use *dhaŋu* and clans such as Djambarrpuyŋu, Liyagawumirr and Djapu use *dhuwal*. These words are indicative of a large range of morphological and phonological differences. Within the Yolŋu languages there are five or six of these larger groupings.

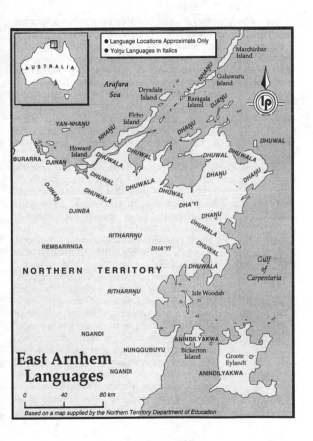

East Arnhem Languages

0   40   80 km

Based on a map supplied by the Northern Territory Department of Education

The Yolŋu languages are surrounded by the non Pama-Nyungan type. From the northwest these are Burarra, Rembarrnga, Ngandi, Nunggubuyu on the mainland and Anindilyakwa, the language of Groote Eylandt. Of course these languages did not divide people – groups within a geographical area intermarry and the children are/ were raised with different languages spoken around the hearth.

In all communities the population is still linguistically diverse. Only one language in the region has no living speakers. The comments following about the most commonly used languages are to be understood in the light of the fact that all communities are still multilingual, although the population of speakers of several varieties is ageing.

The most widely spoken Yolŋu varieties are, moving from the west: Djinaŋ around Ramingining; a Dhuwal variety usually referred to as Djambarrpuyŋu (but somewhat different to the usual Djambarrpuyŋu) from Milingimbi to Gapuwiyak; Dhuwaya a koine (a new Yolŋu language) that has evolved around Yirrkala. At

Numbulwar Kriol is the first language of most young people but there is a major effort being undertaken in the community to maintain other languages, the main one being Nunggubuyu.

Traditional languages and culture are being supported by schools in the region, with and without bilingual programs, through various activities and programs. This has come at an oppurtune time given increasing numbers of Aboriginal teachers, including four principals, and extensive passive understanding of the languages. In bilingual programs, children are formally instructed in English and local languages. Languages of the area have been written since the sixties. The Yolŋu languages share a common orthography but different ones exist for the non-Pama Nyungan languages in the region. Most writing is still associated with schools and bible translation. Bilingual schools have printing facilities so this is where most locally produced material is to be found. Some of these materials are available at local craft shops and newsagencies. Others are to be found as part of the Northern Australian Collection at the State Library of the Northern Territory, 25 Cavenagh St, Darwin.

The Yolŋu have always encouraged people living in their communities to learn their languages. Missions in this region also encouraged staff to learn. The rock band Yothu Yindi is currently the most widely knownrepresentative of this willingness to share. The words yothu (yuuthu) and yindi translate as 'child, young' and 'big, important' respectively. However, in combination they refer to the relationship between mother and child, which extends to the clans, land and ceremony involved. The child's clan has major responsibilities to the mother's clan and members of the rock band are in this relationship to each other. Most communities have their own bands. Yothu Yindi draws its membership from clans associated with the eastern mainland communities of Gunyaŋara (Ski Beach) near Nhulunbuy and Tlikala.

Another popular band in the region, the Wirriŋa band, also has tapes commercially available (through CAAMA). They are a Milingimbi band. Many other communities have local bands. Tapes of local church choirs are also available through local churches.

Further Reading

Cooke, M. 1987 *Makassar and Northeast Arhem Land* (Missing Links and Living Bridges), Batchelor, Batchelor College.

Groote Eyland Linguistics 1993 *Eningerribirra–langwa lurra* (anindilyakwa–English).

Heath, J. 1982 *Nunggubuyu dictionary*, Australian Institute of Aboriginal Studies Canberra.

McConvell, P. *Girindji Grammar* (draft) Unpublished.

MacDonald, E. 1964 'Notes on the Noun Classes of Anyula', *Papers on the Languages of the Australian Aborigines*, AIAS, Canberra.

Urry, J. & Walsh, M. 1981 'The lost 'Macassar language' of northern Australia', *Aboriginal History*, Vol. 5, A.N.U. Press, Canberra.

Walker, A. & Zorc, S. 1981 'Austronesian loanwords in Yolñu-matha languages of north-east Arnhem Land', *Aboriginal History*, Vol. 5, A.N.U. Press, Canberra.

Zorc, D.R. 1986 *Yoinu–Matha Dictionary*, School of Australian Linguistics Batchelor, NT.

Western Australian Languages

Introduction

As in other parts of Australia, there are two broad types of languages in Western Australia. Those which are spoken in the Kimberley roughly north of the Fitzroy River are of the prefixing type, like the languages of the Top End of the Northern Territory. The remainder are non-prefixing. (Prefixes are letters added to the beginning of words, used to distinguish types of words. See the Introduction of this section for more information.) Beyond this major division, a useful way to describe the languages is by region.

The Southwest

A single language, Nyungar, was spoken in the southwest of the state and existed in a number of different dialects. In the early days of contact with Europeans, a large number of loanwords were taken into English. However the effects of European settlement then caused a catastrophic loss of language (and culture), and there are now very few speakers of Nyungar remaining.

The Murchison & Gascoyne

The main surviving language of this region is Wajarri, originally spoken in the Eastern Murchison. While there were a number of different languages spoken in this area, the people all referred to themselves as Yamaji and will say that they speak the Yamaji language. Wajarri is also spoken in Carnarvon where the original languages are essentially moribund. The eastern Wajarri people live in the Western Desert cultural area.

Pilbara

The southern and western Pilbara region, from the Gascoyne to Ashburton rivers formed a cultural area with the languages spoken along the Pilbara coast. The languages of this region also had similarities but sadly few speakers of these languages remain.

A number of languages are still spoken in the northern/eastern Pilbara, the most widely known being Yindjibarndi spoken in Roebourne, Onslow and other Pilbara towns. The Pilbara people form a cultural group sharing similar kinship systems and ritual practices. People travel from Carnarvon in the south, to Jigalong in the east and LaGrange mission in the north for summer ceremonies.

Western Desert

A range of dialects of the same language are spoken across large parts of Western Australia, South Australia and the Northern Territory, extending from the Great Australian Bight, north to the Kimberley and west to the Hamersley ranges and Murchison goldfields.

Kimberley

There were originally about 15 different languages spoken in the Kimberley region, but with a quite high degree of grammatical difference between these languages. The situation here is similar to that in the Northern Territory; while there are eight different language 'families' in the Kimberley, the languages of the remaining areas of West Australia fall into just one of these, the Pama-Nyungan 'family'.

Most Aboriginal people over the age of 30 in the Kimberley, Pilbara and Western Desert regions speak one or more traditional languages. Throughout most of the state, Aboriginal people, except possibly the elderly, speak English. There is an array of varieties of Aboriginal English ranging from close to standard Australian English, through to varieties very close to Kriol (see page 151).

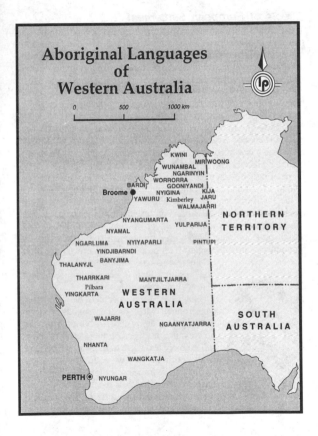

Aboriginal Languages of Western Australia

0   500   1000 km

KWINI   MIRIWOONG
WUNAMBAL
NGARINYIN
WORRORRA
GOONIYANDI
BARDI   NYIGINA   KIJA
Broome   YAWURU   Kimberley   JARU
WALMAJARRI

NORTHERN TERRITORY

NYANGUMARTA   YULPARIJA
NYAMAL
NGARLUMA   NYIYAPARLI   PINTUPI
YINDJIBARNDI
BANYJIMA
THALANYJI
THARRKARI   MANTJILTJARRA
Pilbara
YINGKARTA   WESTERN
AUSTRALIA
SOUTH
AUSTRALIA
WAJARRI
NGAANYATJARRA

NHANTA
WANGKATJA

PERTH   NYUNGAR

Effects of European Settlement

The European settlement of Western Australia began with the establishment of the Swan River colony (Perth) in 1829 and spread to other parts of the state over the next 50 years, with the establishment of pastoral industries in the northwest, pearl fishing on the Pilbara and Kimberley coasts and gold rushes in the Kalgoorlie and Murchison regions. The effects of European settlement on Aboriginal languages has varied from causing the gradual decline in use over a number of generations, to rapid and complete extinction.

Knowledge of the Nyungar language has been gradually declining for 150 years. Today, younger Nyungar people may know little more than a few hundred words, and a handful of phrases. These are used to replace English words in what is otherwise a variety of Aboriginal English (see page 151). The original dialect diversity of Nyungar has been compromised, with virtually nothing remaining of the Perth dialect, and most people using words of the eastern Nyungar areas. English has had an influence on the sound system and grammatical structure of modern Nyungar. The initial nasal sound (**ng** as in 'sing') is not used by younger speakers, who thus pronounce words like *nguup*, 'blood', as *nuup*. Younger speakers

also use word order to distinguish subject and object, rather than the case-marking system of traditional Nyungar.

Language loss in other areas has been more catastrophic. Most of the languages originally spoken along the Ashburton river are now extinct, not because their speakers have shifted more and more to English, but because whole communities were destroyed by the effects of European settlement. The languages did not die, their speakers did.

In some places speakers of different languages were thrown together in organised settlements. Languages have been lost as people shifted to one or two main languages and away from their mother tongues. Yindjibarndi is the most successful survivor of the many languages which came together in Roebourne. In parts of the Kimberley, a new language (called Kriol) using words borrowed mainly from English, but with a sound system and some aspects of grammar taken from traditional languages, grew out of this situation.

Keeping Languages Strong

In recent years, many communities have increased efforts to maintain their languages and in some cases to revive languages which have been lost. An important part of this effort has been the establishment of community language centres which provide general language resource materials. The language centres encourage the interest of members of the general public and welcome visitors.

Until very recently, West Australia has not had a clear policy promoting the teaching of Australian languages in state-run schools and most language teaching or bilingual education programmes have been community based and privately or federally funded. Hopefully there will be an increasing number of state-run programmes in the future and a corresponding increase in awareness of Aboriginal languages in the general non-Aboriginal community.

Language maintenance and revival is closely tied to cultural maintenance and revival and an important aspect of this involves maintaining a spiritual connection to the land. In recent times, communities have sought increased control over their traditional lands; in some areas, people have moved back to their homelands and established 'outstations', in other places Aboriginal community groups hold pastoral leases and so retain access to their land for traditional purposes alongside the use of the land to run stock. Aboriginal rangers are increasingly involved in the management of national parks, and many communities continue to seek their land rights under federal and state law.

Cultural Information

The most important organising principles of Aboriginal society is the kinship system and every member of the community is part of a complex web of kin relations. As well as certain rights and obligations which stem from particular relationships, the system of kin relationships provides a safety net which is used by Aboriginal people when they are in trouble. Even far from home, the web of connections means that a person will be able to find a classificatory 'brother' or 'sister', a friend who will look after them. Aboriginal people travel a lot, and in WA can expect nearly always to be close to 'family'.

The kinship system determines various patterns of social responsibility, many of which require special forms and styles of speaking. Thus there are rules of politeness and avoidance; traditionally, people would avoid their in-laws and use a special vocabulary in speaking with them. Children would defer to members of their parents generation, but interaction between members of the same generation, or between grandparents and grandchildren is more relaxed and often involves a great deal of joking, teasing and innuendo. Aboriginal people do not, as a rule, interrogate each other as English speakers tend to do, but rely on each other to be reasonably cooperative in communicating information.

Visitors can respect these rules of politeness by treating older people with respect and reserve and by understanding that the reserve they may meet from younger people is not necessarily a cool reception. Unless introduced, introduce yourself by first asking from a little distance, 'Can I come and see you?' Aboriginal people, both men and women, always take each other's hand in greeting, with a gentle and not too firm grip. They will usually expect you to introduce yourself first. The names of people recently deceased are avoided for a period of time and in general the overuse of personal names is avoided. People address each other by a kinterm or by nickname.

Direct questions are easily interpreted as rudeness and are more politely phrased as statements of knowledge; 'I'm trying to find my way to the Language Centre'. More generally, if you want to learn something, give something in return. Tell a story/anecdote to hear a story. Don't be too serious, and don't be too surprised to find yourself the butt of a joke. Aboriginal people tend to tolerate more silence in communication than the average Westerner. If no-one says anything for a few minutes, don't feel compelled to fill the silence. Be content to wait and to listen.

As in most cultures, some knowledge is restricted and cannot be discussed freely. Certain rituals and particular sites, certain songs, dances and language styles may be restricted to initiated men.

Some objects, decorations, or graphic designs may also be restricted and cannot be seen by uninitiated men and women.

All Aboriginal sites are protected under law, whether these be rock paintings or carvings, or scatterings of stone tools in a creek bed. It is an offence to disturb or remove artefacts found in the bush. While not all sites are specifically 'sacred sites', the land itself is sacred in the sense that Aboriginal spirituality embraces the land and everything above and below it. For Aboriginal people, the land is the source of their culture – the stories come from the land.

Specific Locations

The legacy of the Nyungar people is clearest to visitors in the host of local names for places, plants and animals found in the southwest. Aboriginal heritage trails giving details of the uses of various plants, the habits of animals, and historical and mythological information can be found in most national parks throughout the area. In the Goldfields, in communities across the Nullarbor Plain and in the desert, and along the Canning Stock Route north to the Kimberley, people speak dialects of the Western Desert language.

In the Pilbara, most travellers will visit the gorges in Karijini, the Hamersley Ranges National Park. This is Panyjima, Kurrama and Yinhawangka country. The Millstream/Chichester Ranges National Park is Kurrama and Yindjibarndi country. Aboriginal rangers from these local groups work in the parks, while local Aboriginal groups organise wilderness tours of Karijini, led by local experts.

In Broome, visitors will come into contact with speakers of Yawuru and probably also Karajarri, a Western Desert language. At Cape Leveque, tourists will most likely meet the sea-going Bardi people. Travellers on the Gibb River road will pass mainly through Ngarinyin country and visitors to the Bungle Bungle National Park, south of Turkey Creek will probably meet speakers of Kija and Jaru. Miriwoong is spoken further to the North, around Kununurra and Lake Argyle on the Ord River.

In the north of the state, especially in the desert, in the Pilbara and Kimberley, Aboriginal people often speak the new language Kriol, or a variety of English known as Aboriginal English.

The Languages

The sound systems of languages of Western Australia are quite similar to one another. Interdental sounds are made with the tongue between the teeth, alveolar with the tongue tip against the ridge behind the upper teeth, retroflex with the tip of the tongue turned back, and palatal with the tongue against the palate. While these sounds are found in almost all of the languages, there are a number of different spelling systems.

The grammatical structures of the languages vary. Nyungar, in the south, does not have complex suffixes and prefixes and, like some Asian languages, relies on sequences of individual words linked together to convey complex meanings and on relatively fixed word order. By contrast, the Kimberley languages have very complicated paradigms of word forms and in some cases a single word can express the content of a whole sentence. Throughout the rest of the state, words involve the addition of suffixes to indicate grammatical information and word order within sentences is often quite free.

Aboriginal people do not usually expect to speak their languages with non-Aboriginal people and in most such situations English is the language of choice. However, travellers who choose to try out a few local names for animals, plants, or places, will convey the message that they are interested in Aboriginal languages and sympathetic to Aboriginal culture (see wordlists).

Aboriginal English is not always easily understood by speakers of other English dialects. Like Kriol, it uses sounds and structures that are borrowed from traditional languages. There are occasionally special pronouns, words borrowed from traditional languages (especially kinterms), and no gender contrasts (*he* and *him* and words like *fella*, may be used for both men and women). Rules for use, politeness and avoidance, are like those of traditional languages. Visitors should not try to speak Kriol or Aboriginal English. Because of the negative connotations of 'pidgin English', such attempts might be seen as patronising and insulting.

Place Names

Partiikunha	Clamina Gorge
Pajinhurrpa	Cossak

Karlayanguyinha	Cowera Gorge
Murlunmunyjurna	Crossing Pool
Mangkurtu	Fortescue River
Karijini	Hamersley Range (National Park)
Pilirripinha	Manyjina Gorge
Japurakunha	Marillana Gorge
Jintawirrina	Millstream St.
Kawuyu	Mt Nicholson
Walkartatharra	Mt Alexander
Pirnayinmurru	Mt Brockman
Punurrunha	Mt Bruce
Mukuriyarra	Mt Murray
Pirtan	Onslow
Kalharramunha	Rio Tinto Gorge
Jajiwurra	Robe River
Yirramakartu	Roebourne, Jubilee Pool
Kartirtikunha	Yampire Gorge
Parrkapinya	Whim Creek
Ngampiku	Wittenoom (Gorge)

The above list is composed of names from the Pilbara. Many place names in the southwest of the state end in -up. These are all original Nyungar names and the ending simply indicates that the word is the name of a place. Some examples of towns with this ending are:

Boyanup	Jerramungup	Nannup
Cowaramup	Kirrup	Porongurup
Dandalup	Kojonup	Quinninup
Dardenup	Manjimup	Wagerup
Gnowangerup	Mungallup	Wokalup

In the wheatbelt, a good number of names end in -n or -ng. These are also Nyungar names. Some towns with this kind of name are:

Burracoppin	Kellerberrin	Popanyinning
Corrigin	Kondinin	Quairading
Cunderdin	Merredin	Tammin
Katanning	Narrogin	Woodanilling

While some of these place names most likely 'meant something' rather than simply being names, it is not possible to know what this was without detailed knowledge of the exact named place and the mythology surrounding it. Resemblances to other Nyungar words is no guarantee of a connection in meaning.

Further Reading

For more information on the culture of particular areas see:

Tilbrook, L. 1983 *Nyungar Tradition: Glimpses of Aborigines of Southwestern Australia 1829-1914*, University of Western Australia Press.

Tonkinson. R. 1991 *The Mardu Aborigines: Living the Dream in Australia's Desert*, Holt, Rinehart and Winston.

Mowarjarli, 1992 *Yorro Yorro*, Magabala Books.

Richards E. & Hudson J. *Walmajarri-English Dictionary* Summer Institute of Linguistics, Darwin.

Languages of Victoria & New South Wales

Introduction

The south-east of Australia, comprising the present-day states of New South Wales and Victoria, was the earliest and most intensively settled mainland area of the European colonies. During settlement the original inhabitants were dispossessed of their land and killed in large numbers through murder, the spread of disease, and the destruction of their environment and means of living. People were also herded onto missions and government settlements, sometimes being forced to live together with their enemies, and their traditional ways of life were prohibited. As a result, the transmission of traditional Aboriginal culture, including language, from one generation to the next was damaged and a great deal of knowledge was lost.

Today, in New South Wales, a few old fluent speakers remain for a small number of languages, including Bundjalung of the north coast around Lismore, and Baagandji, spoken on the Darling River near Wilcannia. No full speakers of a Victorian Aboriginal language are alive, and none of the languages is used as the main means of communication in any community. However, many Aboriginal people carefully preserve some elements of their linguistic heritage, even generations after the last fluent speakers have passed away. Today, words from traditional languages can still be heard in use in Melbourne and Sydney, and especially in country areas of New South Wales and Victoria. These words and expressions serve to declare the identity of Koori and Murri people amongst whom they continue to be used. In many communities there is rising interest in traditional languages and culture and efforts are under way to preserve and maintain the knowledge that remains.

The visitor to New South Wales and Victoria will see evidence

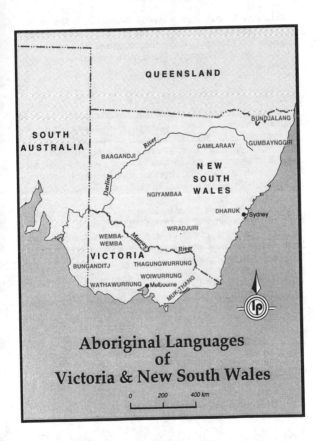

**Aboriginal Languages
of
Victoria & New South Wales**

of traditional Aboriginal languages in three areas: in the continuing use of Aboriginal language words and expressions; in names for places and features of the landscape; and in Aboriginal words that have entered the English language and are in common use by all Australians.

Victoria

The language that covered the area from Melbourne north almost to Echuca on the Murray River is known as Woiwurrung (for the dialect south of the Great Dividing Range) or Thagungwurrung (for the northern dialect). Other important languages of Victoria include Wathawurrung, spoken near Geelong, Wemba-Wemba of the Mallee region, Bunganditj from the south-west corner of Victoria, and Muk Thang, the language of the Ganai (also spelled Kurnai) of Gippsland.

Melbourne was first settled by Europeans in 1835, and within a few years the Aboriginal population was decimated. From 1863 the survivors were placed in a reserve at Coranderrk, near Healesville, and later at other reserves such as Lake Tyers in Gippsland and Framlingham near Warrnambool in the Western District. In the 1960s Luise Hercus carried out an extensive survey of the whole state to record what could be gleaned of the traditional languages – the result was a book containing outline descriptions of three languages from north-western Victoria and adjacent areas of New South Wales, plus word lists for a number of other languages.

For most of the state our knowledge comes from word lists and very brief notes on language structures recorded by settlers, missionaries and explorers over 80 years ago.

In general, Aboriginal words tend to end in vowels, but a feature of Victorian languages is the use of a wide variety of consonants at the end of words. This is reflected in some of the plant names borrowed into English from Victorian languages, and in placenames. For example, we have Cherry Ballart (Native Cherry), Murrnong or Myrnong (Yam-daisy), and places such as Koo-wee-rup and Gariwerd. The latter is an Aboriginal name that has been reintroduced as an alternative name for The Grampians, a mountain range in western Victoria. For many placenames it is impossible to give an exact meaning because of the lack of reliable information; however, the following are some names where the meaning is clear:

Allambee	mishearing of *ngalambi* 'to remain, dwell'; town near Yarragon, Gippsland; also Yallambie, a suburb of Melbourne
Boort	'smoke'; town in Mallee, north-western Victoria
Coranderrk	Victorian Christmas bush; near Healesville
Korrumburra	'march fly'; town in Gippsland
Lara	'stone'; town north of Geelong
Leongatha	'our teeth'; town in Gippsland
Mirboo	'kidney'; town in Gippsland
Narre Warren	'red'; suburb south-east of Melbourne
Wollert	'possum'; town north of Melbourne
Wonthaggi	'fetch!'; town on the Gippsland coast

The following are some other words in Victorian languages that have entered the English language: bunyip (a mythical swamp–dwelling creature), yabby (a crustacean), cumbungi (bulrush), dillon bush (a plant), lerp (a form of scale), lowan (mallee fowl), and tuan (gliding possum).

New South Wales

Current knowledge of the traditional languages of New South Wales is much richer than that which has been salvaged in Victoria. Around Sydney and the central coast, which was settled by Europeans from 1788, the only available information is from 18th and 19th century records, mainly short word lists. However for a number of other languages, especially those of inland New South Wales and the north coast, there are tape recordings, grammars and dictionaries compiled by linguists who worked with the last generation of fluent speakers.

Languages for which there is a deal of reliable information available include Bundjalung and Gumbaynggir (north coast), Gamilaraay (also spelled Kamilaroi), Ngiyambaa (or Wangaaybuwan) and Wiradjuri (north-west and central NSW), and Baagandji (or Paakantyi) (far west). Speakers of some of these languages remain and there are efforts under way in Aboriginal com-

munities to revive and preserve linguistic and cultural heritage. Recently several excellent practical dictionaries and word books of New South Wales languages have appeared – these are listed in the further reading section at the end of this chapter. For further information the visitor is advised to contact local Aboriginal land councils, language centres and schools to discuss studies that are currently being undertaken.

Throughout New South Wales, as in Victoria, there are numerous placenames that have an Aboriginal origin. For many of these it is possible to give an interpretation of their literal meaning (although the significance of these names in the mythology and culture is often not available). Here are some examples giving the original pronunciation and meaning:

Boggabilla	*bagaaybila* – 'place full of creeks'
Bundarra	*bundaarra* – 'place of kangaroos'
Cobar	*gubarr* – 'red ochre'
Coonamble	*gunambil* – 'full of excrement'
Gunnedah	*gunithaa* – 'orphan'
Nambucca	*bagabaga* – 'knees'
Torrowotto	*thuru-katu* – 'snake's windbreak'
Uralla	*urala* – 'camp'
Wagga Wagga	*waagan-waagan* – 'crows'
Woolgoolga	*wiigulga* – 'black fig tree'

Many dozens of words from New South Wales' languages are now at home in general Australian English, especially for the names of plants and animals that were new to the first European settlers. These include:

- birds, such as: galah, kookaburra, brolga, currawong, budgerigar
- animals, such as: dingo, koala, wallaby, wallaroo
- plants, such as: mulga, coolabah, gidgee, bindi-eye
- features of the landscape and Aboriginal artefacts, such as: billabong (river pool), gibber (stone), coolamon (bark dish), woomera (spear-thrower), nulla-nulla (club), gunya (shelter)

Further Reading

The following are some introductory books that deal with Victorian and New South Wales Aboriginal languages. For more infor-

mation contact: Australian Institute of Aboriginal and Torres
Strait Islander Studies, GPO Box 553, Canberra. ACT 0200.

Austin, P. 1992 *A dictionary of Gamilaraay, northern New South Wales* La Trobe University.

Austin, P. 1993 *A reference dictionary of Gamilaraay, northern New South Wales* La Trobe University.

Blake, B.J. 1991 'Woiwurrung: the Melbourne language' in R.M.W. Dixon & B.J. Blake (eds) *The Handbook of Australian Languages, Volume 4* Oxford University Press.

Crowley, T. 1978 *The middle Clarence dialects of Bandjalang*. Australian Institute of Aboriginal and Torres Strait Islander Studies.

Dixon, R.M.W., W.S. Ramson & M. Thomas 1990 *Australian Aboriginal Words in English*. Oxford University Press.

Donaldson, T. 1980 *Ngiyambaa: the language of the Wangaaybuwan*. Cambridge University Press.

Eades, D. 1981 'Gumbaynggir' in R.M.W. Dixon & B.J. Blake (eds) *The Handbook of Australian Languages, Volume 1*. Australian National University Press.

Hercus, L.A. 1982 *The Bagandji language* Pacific Linguistics.

Hercus, L.A. 1986 *Victorian languages: a late survey* Pacific Linguistics.

Hercus, L.A. 1993 *Paakantyi dictionary* Canberra.

Hosking, D. and S. McNicol. 1993 *Wiradjuri* Canberra.

Sharpe, M. 1992 *Dictionary of Western Bundjalung* University of New England.

Sharpe, M. 1993 'Bundjalung: teaching a disappearing language' in M. Walsh & C. Yallop (eds) *Language and culture in Aboriginal Australia* Australian Institute of Aboriginal and Torres Strait Islander Studies.

Torres Strait Languages

Introduction

There are three Torres Strait Islander languages spoken by an Australian indigenous group of some 30,000 people, a large majority of whom are Melanesian people. The rest are of European, Asian and Aboriginal background. Their homelands are a group of small islands scattered along the waterway known as Torres Strait, between the tip of Cape York and Papua New Guinea.

Two of the Torres Strait Islander languages are original indigenous languages. They are Kala Lagaw Ya (KLY), spoken by the people of the western islands of Saibai, Dauan, Boigu, Mabuiag, Badu, Moa (Kubin) and Narupai, and the central islands of Masig, Purma, Yam and Warraber; and Meriam Mir (MM), spoken by the people from eastern islands of Mer, Erub and Ugar. Kala Lagaw Ya is believed to be related to Australian Aboriginal Languages. Meriam Mir on the other hand belongs to the TransFly family of languages along the Papuan coast.

The third traditional language of Torres Strait Islanders is an English-based creole, called Torres Strait Broken (TSB). It is an established *lingua franca*, mainly spoken in the Eastern and Central Islands and Thursday Island, and is the first language of most people there who were born after WW II.

About 6000 Torres Strait Islanders who live in the Torres Strait continue to use the languages and keep them strong. The remaining 80% of Torres Strait Islanders have moved to the provincial towns and cities in the mainland of Australia for various reasons, mainly in search of jobs, good health and better education for their children. Most Torres Strait Islanders who decided to move to the mainland have settled in the coastal towns and cities of Queensland.

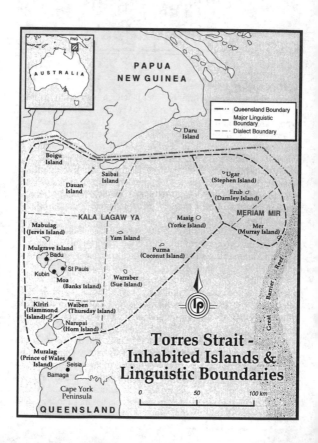

Despite total exposure to the dominant western culture and English language, Torres Strait Islanders on the mainland have managed exceptionally well to maintain their traditional languages.

Kala Lagaw Ya has about 3000 speakers while Meriam Mir speakers are numbered close to 2000; and all Torres Strait Islanders speak Torres Strait Broken regardless of where they live in Australia.

In the Torres Strait today, people on central and eastern islands as well as on Thursday, Horn and Hammond Islands, use Torres Strait Broken on a daily basis, although most adults maintain their traditional indigenous languages. On Boigu, Saibai, Dauan, Mabuiag, Badu, Kubin, Seisia and Bamaga, Kala Lagaw Ya all have regular speakers. Meriam Mer on Murray Island is primarily spoken by adults. Thursday Island is a town with a mixed community of European, Asian and Aboriginal people. English is an official language and is used extensively in government offices, schools, churches, hospital and shops etc. While the two indigenous languages are often used by the speakers amongst themselves, Torres Strait Broken is the most commonly used language on Thursday Island.

European Contact

European contact has had devastating effects on the languages and culture of Torres Strait Islanders. The colonisation process and the cruel policies of assimilation, segregation and integration have greatly contributed to the marginalisation of Torres Strait Islander culture and languages. Official limitations were placed on the use of indigenous languages in schools and public places.

The impact of colonisation resulted in the creation of Torres Strait Broken as a new language in the area. It has developed mainly from the Pacific Island pidgin called Bislama which was brought to Torres Strait by Pacific Islanders who came to the area as labourers in the marine industry.

Interactions between Pacific Islanders, Torres Strait Islanders and other nationals who had migrated to the area, such as Japanese, Malayans and Chinese, resulted in the emergence of Torres Strait Broken which is now distinctly different from the Bislama as spoken today.

Torres Strait Islanders living on the mainland continue to use their traditional languages, despite the total exposure to English language and the Australian way of life.

Community & Cultural Life

The fundamental aspects of the original Torres Strait Islander culture have remained in tact, despite colonisation. However, since the time of initial contact, the dominance of European culture and the influence of other cultures that the Torres Strait Islanders came in contact with, have forced some changes to various aspects of the Torres Strait Islanders' culture. Thus it has been somehow modified and in some instances impoverished, although today, Torres Strait Islanders are still able to practise an enriched and unique cultural way of life.

The most notable cultural trait that Torres Strait Islanders on all islands have hung on to so tightly apart from their languages is their traditional dance. There are different styles of traditional dance which can be performed while standing upright stamping both feet, or in a sitting position. Both forms of dancing require a lot of hand movements and jumping. The dancers usually wear special costumes, depending on what the dance is about. To perform the dances the men wear a piece of cloth called *lava-lava* and a singlet, while women wear specially-made floral dresses. Also, the dancers equip themselves with special regalia consisting of grass-skirt, headress, headbands, necklaces, arm and leg bands and models representing the subject that the dance portrays. All dances are usually accompanied by singing and the pulsating rhythm of drums.

In May of each year, Thursday Island hosts the Torres Strait Cultural Festival. This is designed to promote and strengthen cultural identity. The activities of the Cultural Festival include traditional dance, traditional and contemporary singing, and stalls where people sell food, handicrafts, artefacts and carvings of all description.

Over the years, Torres Strait Islanders have developed a lifestyle suited to their environment. At one time they depended almost entirely on the sea for food and to travel from one island to the next. On land, they cultivated crops in their gardens and domesticated animals, mainly pigs. These days not much gardening is being carried out. Torres Strait Islanders rely more and more on community stores that provide general groceries, including fresh vegetables, fruit and meat. Fish is the staple food, and is caught by handlines and nets or hand spears, and it is supplement with rice, yam, sweet potatoes and taro. The important sources of seafood are dugong and

turtle. Using traditional methods, Torres Strait Islanders spear them with a special harpoon. Because dugong and turtle are considered a luxury, people only eat them on special occasions like weddings and tombstone unveilings.

For special occasions, Torres Strait Islanders hold traditional feasts which include dancing, singing and lots of food. Traditional food requires a lot of preparation. One of the popular traditional foods is *sop-sop*, a mixture of vegetables chopped into small pieces and cooked in coconut cream. In just about every feast, food is cooked in an earth oven or *kap mauri*. The food for *kap mauri* is prepared and wrapped then placed on hot stones lying on the bottom of the pit specially dug in the ground. Any kind of food may be cooked in the *kap mauri* including vegetables, pig, dugong, turtle and damper.

Tombstone unveiling is one of the important family events celebrated with a big traditional feast. It involves a lot of preparation by the family of the deceased person. The preparations include the collecting of money from each member of the family, erecting a tombstone on the grave and putting on a feast.

The outer island communities are changing fairly rapidly from traditional village settings to small townships. All the islands now have modern houses, schools, medical facilities, telephones and electricity. However, in general, life on the islands is at a notably leisurely pace. The daily activities of the people revolve around family and community affairs.

Torres Strait Islanders are devout Christians. Most of them are Anglicans. Some islands have smaller churches of other denominations. They worship every Sunday in churches built by themselves. Church services are normally conducted in English but most of the hymns are sung in their own languages. An important religious event that people throughout the Torres Strait celebrate on 1 July each year, is the festival of the 'Coming of the Light'. This event signifies the arrival of the missionaries of the London Missionary Society in the Torres Strait in 1871. The festival is usually celebrated with a church service followed by a re-enactment of how the people on each island greeted the missionaries. In the re-enactment, some people dress as the missionaries while others dress in warrior costumes.

The main authorities in an island community are the community council chairperson and the councillors, the priest and the clan elders. Visitors are expected to observe cultural protocol when visiting the islands. It is therefore important to find out as much as possible beforehand.

Specific Locations

The places that are visited most frequently by outsiders are Bamaga, Seisia and Thursday Island. In winter, tourists travel by road to Cape York and camp in the camping area at Seisia. A regular ferry operates from Thursday Island, to service the Northern Peninsula Area communities, on most days of the week.

Thursday Island is the commercial and administrative centre for Torres Strait. It has a fasinating history. The fort is one of the main attractions on Thursday Island. On Green Hill there are sixteen inch guns which were build at the turn of the century in fear of a Russian invasion that never eventuated. Thursday Island is surrounded by a number of islands clustered together. The airport is on Horn Island. The airlines provide regular ferry services to and from Thursday Island.

All the islands not included in the Muralag (Prince of Wales) group, including Thursday Island, are referred to as outer islands. To visit any of the outer islands, it is important to make an arrangement with the Council of the island because of limited accommodation.

Dialects of KLY & MM

Kala Lagaw Ya (KLY)

Kala Lagaw Ya is a language with four dialects: the Kala Kawaw Ya (KKY) of the islands of Saibai, Dauan and Boigu; Mabuiag (M) of Mabuiag Island and Badu; Kaurareg (K) of Kubin (Moa) and Nurapai (Horn Island).

The differences between these dialects are minimal and lie mainly in words and sounds.

Meriam Mir (MM)

Meriam Mir had two dialects and the differences between them were restricted to words and sounds. Only Mer dialect has survived.

Variation in Torres Strait Broken (TSB)

The way Eastern Islanders and Central/Western Islanders speak TSB varies in terms of the vocabulary used, the different words being derived from their indigenous languages.

Awa, yumi go.	'Uncle, let's go.'	Eastern
Awadhe, yumi go.	'Uncle, let's go.'	Central/Western

Sounds/Pronunciation

Vowels

The vowels in the three Torres Strait Islander languages resemble those of English.

The simple vowels are:

a	as in 'but'
e	as in 'pet'
i	as in 'bit'
o	as in 'pot'
u	as in 'put'

The vowel clusters are:

ei	as in 'pay'
ai	as in 'bite'
oi	as in 'toy'
au	as in 'now'
eu	pronounced like 'milk' in cockney English

Kala Lagaw Ya has an additional vowel schwa ' ə ' and semi-vowels **y** and **w**. The orthography of the three languages differs when writing the vowel clusters. In KLY, **i** is replaced with a semi-vowel **y** and **u** with a semi-vowel **w** when followed by another vowel, eg. The semi-vowels in KKY dialect are also used as glides which can be inserted in between the vowel cluster **ia**.

Consonants

All the Torres Strait languages have the consonant sounds: **b**, **d**, **g**, **j**, **k**, **l**, **m**, **n**, **p**, **r**, **s**, **t**, **w**, **y** and **z**, as in English. Kala Lagaw Ya has three additional consonant sounds, **dh** as in 'the', **ng** as in 'swing' and **th** as in 'thin'.

Pronouns

	KLY	MM	TSB
I	*ngay* (intr.); *ngath* (tr.)	*kaka*	*ai*
you	*ngi*(intr.); *ngidh* (tr.) *ni* (intr.) (M & K); *nidh* (M & K)	*mama*	*yu*
she	*na* (intr.); *nadh* (tr.)	*neur*	*em*
he	*nuy* (intr.) *nuydh* (tr.)	*makrem*	*em*
we (two, exc.)	*ngalbe; ngalbay* (M & K)	*mimi*	*mitu*
we (two, inc.)	*ngoeba; ngaba* (M & K)	*eaka*	*yumtu*
you (two)	*ngipel; nipel* (M & K)	*kiki*	*yutu*
they (two)	*palay*	*gairle*	*dhemtu*
we (exc. they & I, not you)	*ngoey*	*mimi*	*mipla*
we (inc. we & you)	*ngalpa*	*mimi*	*yumpla*
you	*ngitha; nitha* (M & K)	*kikiama*	*yupla*
they	*thana*	*gairle*	*dhempla*

Useful Words & Phrases

	KLY	MM	TSB
Yes	*Wa*	*Baru*	*Wa*
No	*Lawnga*	*Nole*	*No*
Welcome.	*Sew ngapa.*	*Maiem.*	*Maiem*
Goodbye.	*Yawa.* (KKY)	*Yawo.*	*Si yu* or *Yawo.*

Greetings & Civilities
Kala Lagaw Ya (KLY)

How are you?	*Ngi midh?* (KKY); *Ni midhikidh?* (M & K)
Fine.	*Balabayginga.* (KKY)
	Matha mina. (M & K)
Have you eaten?	*Ngi aydu purathima a?* (KKY)
	Ni aydun purthema a? (M)
	Ni aydun purthema? (K)
I have eaten already.	*Ngath aygud mu-asin.* (KKY)
	(m) *Ngaw aygud mina-asin.* (M & K)
	(f) *Nguzu aygud mina-asin.* (M & K)
I have not eaten yet.	*Ngay aydu purthayginga.* (KKY)
	(m) *Ngaw ayngu purthayginga.* (M & K)
	(f) *Nguzu ayngu purthayginga.* (M & K)
Come inside the house!	*Aya, ngapa lagiya muyari!* (KKY)
	Aye, ngapa mudhiya uth! (M & K)
Thank you.	*Eso.* (KKY, M & K)
Very good.	*Mina boelbayginga.* (KKY)
	Matha mina. (M)
	Matha mina. (K)

Meriam Mir (MM)

How are you?	*Nako manali?*
Fine.	*Sikakanali*
Have you eaten?	*Aka ma lewer erwe?*
I have eaten already.	*Kai emethu lewer erwe?*
I have not eaten yet.	*Ka nole lewer erwe?*
Come inside the house!	*Ma thaba bau mithem.*
Thank you.	*Eswau.*
Very good	*Dhobo kaine.*

Torres Strait Broken (TSB)

How are you?	*Wis wei (yu)?*
Fine.	*Orait.*
Have you eaten?	*U bi kaikai?*
I have eaten already.	*Ai bi pinis kaikai.*
I have not eaten yet.	*Ai no bi kaikai.*
Come inside the house!	*Kam insaid hous!*
Thank you.	*Eso po yu.*
Very good.	*Prapa gud.*

Traditional Life & Crafts

	KLY	MM	TSB
church	*Yoewth* (KKY)	*Zogo metha*	*Sos*
	Maygi mudh (M & K)	*Meb*	*mun*
moon	*moelpal* KKY)		
	kisay (M & K)		
God	*Augadh* (KKY, M & K)	*Ople*	*God*

Holy spirit	*Maygi mari* (KKY) *Maygi mar* (M & K)	*Lamar zogo*	*Oli Gos*
priest	*misnare* (KKY & K) *niyay kaz* (M)	*Bab*	*pris*
drum	*burubur* (KKY) *warup* (M & K)	*Warup*	*dram*

Directions & the Countryside

Is that path good? MM: *Able gab debele eki?*

Not so good. MM: *Nole able adud gab eki.*

	KLY	MM	TSB
beside	*pasinu*	*meke*	*klustun*
path	*yabugud*	*kebi gab*	*rod*
right	*gethadoegam*	*pedike*	*rait*
left side	*boedhadhoegam*	*kemer pek*	*lep said*
above	*gimal*	*kotho*	*antap*
below	*apal*	*sep*	*andanith*
in front	*parunu*	*kikem*	*prant*
behind	*kalanu*	*keubu*	*biyain*
fire	*muy*	*ur*	*paya*
hill	*pad*	*paser*	*il*
river	*koesa*	*-riba*	
rock	*kula*	*bakir*	*ston*
smoke	*thu*	*kemur*	*smok*
sun	*goeygalim*	*san*	
tree	*puy*	*lu*	*tri*

People & Animals

	KLY	MM	TSB
person	*mabayg*	*le*	*man*
friend	*igalayg* (KKY)	*kimeg*	*pren*
	thubudh (M & K)		
man	*gargaz* (KKY)	*kimiar*	*man*
	garka (M & K)		
woman	*yoepkaz* (KKY)	*kosker*	*oman*
	ipika (M & K)		
old man	*kulba thathi* (KKY)	*au le*	*ol man*
	koey kaz (M & K)		
old woman	*kulba apu* (KKY)	*au kosker*	*ol oman*
	koey kaz (M & K)		
baby	*mapeth* (KKY)	*kebi werem*	*beibi*
	moekaz (M)		
	moegikaz (K)		
dog	*umay*	*omai*	*dog*
cat	*pusi*	*pusi*	*pusi*
rat	*makas*	*mukeis*	*rat*
snake	*thabu* (KKY)	*tabo*	*sneik*
	thab (M & K)		

Further Reading

At present, there is only one publication on Torres Strait Broken. It is in a book called *Broken (Introduction to the Creole Language of the Torres Strait)* by Anna Shnukal, 1988. This is primarily a dictionary, which also contains the grammar of Torres Strait Islander Broken. As for the two indigenous languages of Torres Strait, there are a number of unpublished materials available which can be researched through libraries. There is an article on a sketched grammar, and a short word list on Kalaw Kawa Ya, published in *Languages in Australia*, edited by Suzanne Romaine. The article is by Kevin Ford & Dana Ober and is called *A Sketch of Kalaw Kawaw Ya*.

For more information about Torres Strait Islander culture and lifestyle, see *Torres Strait Islanders: Custom and Colonialism* by Jeremy Beckett (Cambridge University Press, Cambridge, 1987) or the two books by Lindsay Wilson, *Thathilgaw Emeret Lu* and *Kerkar Lu*.

PLANET TALK

Lonely Planet's FREE quarterly newsletter

We love hearing from you and think you'd like to hear from us.

When...*is the right time to see reindeer in Finland?*
Where...*can you hear the best palm-wine music in Ghana?*
How...*do you get from Asunción to Areguá by steam train?*
What...*should you leave behind to avoid hassles with customs in Iran?*

*For the answer to these and
many other questions read
PLANET TALK.*

Every issue is packed with up-to-date travel news and advice including:

- *a letter from Lonely Planet founders Tony and Maureen Wheeler*
- *travel diary from a Lonely Planet author - find out what it's really like
  out on the road*
- *feature article on an important and topical travel issue*
- *a selection of recent letters from our readers*
- *the latest travel news from all over the world*
- *details on Lonely Planet's new and forthcoming releases*

To join our mailing list contact any Lonely Planet office.
LONELY PLANET PUBLICATIONS
Australia: PO Box 617, Hawthorn, Victoria 3122 (tel: 03-819 1877)
USA: 155 Filbert Street, Suite 251, Oakland, CA 94607 (tel: 510-893 8555)
UK: 10 Barley Mow Passage, Chiswick, London W4 4PH (tel: 081-742 3161)
FRANCE: 71 bis, rue du Cardinal Lemoine – 75005 Paris (tel: 1-46 34 00 58)

Also available Lonely Planet T-Shirts. 100% heavy weight cotton (S, M, L, XL)